FROM THE ANGLO-SAXONS TO THE VIKINGS

FROM THE ANGLO-SAXONS TO THE VIKINGS

HISTORY, MYSTERY AND MYTH

ANETTE GULDAGER BOYE

PEN & SWORD HISTORY

AN IMPRINT OF PEN & SWORD BOOKS LTD.
YORKSHIRE – PHILADELPHIA

First published in Great Britain in 2026 by
PEN AND SWORD HISTORY
An imprint of
Pen & Sword Books Ltd
Yorkshire – Philadelphia

Print ISBN 978 1 03611 491 6
ePUB ISBN 978 1 03611 493 0
ePDF ISBN 978 1 03611 495 4

A CIP catalogue record for this book is available from the British Library.

Typeset in Times New Roman 10.5/13.5 by
SJmagic DESIGN SERVICES, India.
Printed and bound in the UK by CPI Group (UK) Ltd.

The Publisher's authorised representative in the EU for product safety is Authorised Rep Compliance Ltd., Ground Floor, 71 Lower Baggot Street, Dublin D02 P593, Ireland.
www.arccompliance.com

For a complete list of Pen & Sword titles please contact
PEN & SWORD BOOKS LIMITED
George House, Units 12 & 13, Beevor Street, Off Pontefract Road,
Barnsley, South Yorkshire, S71 1HN, England
E-mail: enquiries@pen-and-sword.co.uk
Website: www.pen-and-sword.co.uk

or

PEN AND SWORD BOOKS
1950 Lawrence Rd, Havertown, PA 19083, USA
E-mail: uspen-and-sword@casematepublishers.com
Website: www.penandswordbooks.com

MIX
Paper | Supporting responsible forestry
FSC® C013604

Contents

Acknowledgements ... vii
Introduction ... viii

1 Folklore in Daily Life ... 1
2 What Lies in a Name ... 3
3 Animal and Human Sacrifice ... 7
4 Pagan 'Holy' Places ... 11
5 Water as a Gateway to the Transcendent ... 15
6 Animism ... 19
7 The Völva ... 20
8 Seidr ... 25
9 Galdr, Runes, Sorcery, and Swords ... 28
10 The Fylgja in the Norse World. ... 34
11 The Gods of the Germanic Tribes. ... 38
12 Other Female Goddesses / Spirits of the Norse Myths ... 48
13 Skalds, Scops and the Tul or Thul (Poet/Wise Man) ... 52
14 Festivals in the Norse World ... 57
15 Snakes and Serpents in the Norse World ... 61
16 The Horse in the Norse World ... 71
17 Wolves in the Norse World ... 75

18 Boars, Hogs, and Pigs in Norse Mythology 82
19 Goats in Norse Mythology 86
20 Shapeshifting 88
21 The Number Nine and Three 95
22 The Álfar/Fairies 102
23 The Fairy/Elves Cup 109
24 The Fairy Rings 113
25 Burial Mounds and Natural Hills as Fairy Ground 115
26 Hobgoblins, Goblins, Brownies, and the Scandinavian 'Nisse' or 'Tomte' 120
27 Changelings 129
28 Means by Which You Could Avoid Malignant Sorcery 137
29 Will-o'-the-Wisp, Ellylldan 140
30 Selkie, Seal Folk and the Mermaids, Water Spirits 142
31 The Kelpies 155
32 The Ravens 163
33 Trees 169
34 Black Spectral Dogs in Folklore, the Barghest 184

References 189
Bibliography 198

Acknowledgements

I want to express a thank you to my family for their patience as I have dived into old stories and sources for hours. Without their support I could not have undertaken this project. Also, a heartfelt thank you to Brian Edwards for his help with the English language. He has played a great part in how this book has taken form. As my native language is Danish his help has been invaluable.

Introduction

This book sets out to tell readers about folklore in Britain and wider Europe by examining ancient myth and legends, with the focus on Britain's Germanic myth and folklore. These myths and legends are pre- and concurrent with the Christian era, and cover a wide mix of social groups, whose boundaries were often in a state of flux. It will therefore consider, with examples, types of beliefs held both within and outside formal religion and at the same time, scrutinise the shifting roles of religious officials and authorities both within and beyond ecclesiastical boundaries as they sought to reconcile their orthodoxy of Pagan beliefs and practice. It will do this by tracing the history of folklore back to the original faith of the population in question, in this case the Anglo-Saxons, the Norse, and the Germanic tribes

Folklore in Britain and across Europe is even today a mix of pre-Christian beliefs, myth, and legends that merged with Christianity, and some of the most significant days and festivals celebrated by the Church actually stem from pre-Christian social practice. In the early days of Christianity, the Church wanted people to convert, so adopting an important celebration or specific tradition from the pre-Christian era was a way to encourage them to do so. At the same time, however, outside the established religious system, there have always been parallel folk beliefs often tied to objects or forces in nature.

The Church in the Middle Ages was relatively open to incorporating elements from the Pagan faith. In addition to what was otherwise expected of the priest within the framework of the Church, he also took care of magical rituals such as, for example, to ensure fertility and prosperity. But this presented problems because, as time went on, the Church wanted these traditions rooted out. This became particularly apparent after the Reformation in the sixteenth century, when the use of magical remedies and rhymes became increasingly frowned upon by the Church. After the Reformation, the Catholic Church and other reformed Churches began to consider magical rhymes, chants, and beliefs in Otherworldly beings outside of the established faith to be heretical.

It is in this light that we can look at folklore, myth, and legends through time. In many ways the old beliefs and practices continued to exist but changed in shape, form and content due to new events that emerged. Folk beliefs are not static. They change in form, both positively and negatively, having a more popular base in society and at the same time existing in a less regulated environment than official belief systems. This is one reason why we have so many traditions across Europe, which are both similar and yet inherently different because they sometimes have a local twist not seen elsewhere.

And in some places, the picture is more blurred than in others. For example, in some areas of England you have the influence of beliefs from the Celts, the Romans, and various immigrants from the Germanic tribes. First came the arrival of the Saxons, Angles and Jutes and later the Danes or Norse (often today known as the 'Vikings'). In Scotland, Ireland and Wales, the Celtic influence is obvious and to a lesser extent, so is the Norse influence from Norwegian and Danish groups. What makes the picture even more complicated is the fact that Celtic and Germanic beliefs are often similar, so distinguishing between them can be very difficult.

These various tribes also influenced each other, and customs and beliefs passed back and forth between different groups. This book will look at early tribes such as the Anglo-Saxons, Jutes and the Norse throughout the British Isles, to follow the journey of myths and folklore throughout the ages, up to modern times.

The Germanic Tribes and Anglo-Saxons

The Germanic tribes were of Indo-European origin. The Indo-European peoples have a common ancestry and linguistically they are related; their cultures have some common features, as do their beliefs.

When it comes to Britain, the Germanic people came as one of the later arrivals, although a recent DNA study proves that Scandinavians also crossed into what was to become England during the Roman period. This study has proven that one Roman gladiator was in fact twenty-five per cent Scandinavian.

Incursion to what became the English Island started before the collapse of this part of the Roman Empire in the early fifth century. From the middle of the third century, raiders from what was called Germania, belonging to a tribe called the Saxons, had started striking the southern and eastern coast of Britain, though it would take a while before full scale immigration took place.

In the fourth century the Picts arrived. Later, came the attacks from Ireland. The Roman Empire had come under pressure from all sides, being plagued by Pictish and Scottish raiders and, from the south, Saxon incursion.

The Anglo-Saxons settled in the fifth and early sixth centuries in what was, until fairly recently, mistakenly known as the Dark Ages. This period was initially known thus due to a scarcity of historical records, but the amount of scholastic research undertaken in recent decades has transformed our understanding of the period, which is now better termed as the Early Middle Ages. The details of the arrival and settlement of the Anglo-Saxons on English soil is beyond the scope of this book, but suffice it to say that they brought with them a new set of beliefs from the Germanic world. By this time, a large area of Britain inside the Roman empire had for some time been converted to Christianity. Much of the country had been Romanised and therefore the Romano/British culture was the one prevalent in the area. At first the invading Saxons and other immigrants from continental Europe and Scandinavia had kept their old faith, swearing to Wotan (Odin) and Thor, but by the seventh century the Anglo-Saxons had also converted to Christianity, giving their allegiance to the Pope in Rome. But along with its newly found Christianity, the areas populated by the Anglo-Saxons saw the rise of new kingdoms and warlike kings trying to take control of neighbouring areas. It is during this time period that a king or warlord was put to rest at the now famous burial site of Sutton Hoo, in what was East Anglia. This Anglo-Saxon burial demonstrates that the English people, although now under the control of Rome, had not entirely let go of their old burial customs, especially those that indicated status. Yet, as a whole, the country had by then largely converted to Christianity. Mark Morris points to King Rædwald as a possible candidate for the high-status burial in the mound at Sutton Hoo. He states:

> Admittedly we cannot say for sure that this was Rædwald's treasure – his body was absent, erased by acid like the occupant of the tomb of Prittlewell.[1]

The Vikings

It has been suggested that the East Anglian realm, of which little written material survives, had likely produced the same amount of written material as the rest of the country but that material may have been destroyed as a result of the Viking Conquest, including the arrival, in AD 865, of the Great Heathen Army which was comprised mostly of Danes and was supposedly led by the sons of the renowned Ragnar Lodbrog. To go into Ragnar's legend here is too extensive a task, but as with the legendary King Arthur, his story is embedded in popular myth and brimming with serpents and dragons, portraying a man larger than life. The Heathen Army brought with them to England the old beliefs that the Anglo-Saxons had left behind when converting to Christianity.

In the eighth century, in continental Europe, we hear of several missionaries of Anglo-Saxon origin. One such is Willibrord who, with his men, cut down Donar's Oak, a sacred tree dedicated to Donar or Thor in Hesse, in today's Germany. When the Pagan shrine had been cut down, the oak's wood was used for a church. This very same missionary visited the Danish King Angantyr in around the year AD 710.

Willibrord described the Danish King Angantyr as 'more savage than any beast and harder than stone', because he was not a Christian and refused to convert. Orgendus in Latin, or Angantyr in Danish, is possibly the king who founded Ribe as a trading town and had the Canhaven Canal constructed at Samsø. Perhaps he also strengthened 'Dannevirke', a fortification stretching thirty kilometres across Jutland in what is today's northern Germany and until 1864 part of Denmark.

In AD 772 the Saxon wars began on the Continent. This series of wars led to the forced conversion of the continental Saxons by Charlemagne. This brought the Frankish Empire to the border of the Danes. The Danes were the allies of the Saxons, and the Danish king, Godofredus (Latin, or Gudrød/Gudfred in Danish) actively fought the Franks until he was murdered in AD 810.

Widukind, a Saxon nobleman and rebel, was said to have been related to the king of the Danes through marriage. It is uncertain, however, whether his wife was a sister or daughter of the Danish king, Sigfred, who ruled prior to AD 777 to sometime after AD 798. Sigfred was king prior to Godofredus and very possibly his father, though we do not know the exact relationship between the two. What we do know is that Godofredus took over immediately after Sigfred and that the kings usually were selected among someone from the royal line. Most often it was the son of the previous king, and it need not be the eldest. The new king would be selected according to his suitability for the position.

Godofredus's son, Horik I, later took over after a conflict with other contestants for the throne. In Horik's reign many fleets attacked around Europe. Godofredus was the Danish king that destroyed the trading town of Reric and founded Haithabu. The Danish kingdom at this time seems to have been comprised of what is today's Denmark, northern Germany to the border at Dannevirke, Scania in today's Sweden and what was known as Vestfold in Norway. Vestfold, as part of the Danish king's realm, is mentioned in Frankish sources, when Harald Klak and Reginfred, co-kings and brothers, had to go there to quell a rebellion around AD 813, at the far outermost part of their kingdom. The later King Horik I and his brothers took advantage of this rebellion, pushed out this other branch of the Danish royal house and re-established the line of Godofredus.

King Horik I was co-king several times, thus also with Harald Klak, who was eventually overthrown in AD 827. Harald Klak was the first Danish king to be christened. Supposedly, Ragnar Lodbrok was said to have helped Horik I and his brothers to take control of the Danish kingdom, or parts of it at least. Co-kings and sea-kings were not an unusual phenomenon in Scandinavia at this time. (Sea-kings were a leader of a fleet that had a substantial number of ships and men under them.) Sometimes these also became land-kings. According to Frankish sources, a Reginherus (Ragnar in Norse) conducted raids along Seinen. He was paid to leave Paris in AD 845, before later visiting the court of Horik I, boasting about his exploits, and it is here that he reportedly died of a plague. At least that is what we are told in the Frankish sources, from where he is best known.

This Reginherus is believed by many historians to be the real Ragnar Lodbrok, including this author. The very same year a large fleet sailed up the Elbe and burned down Hamburg; the mission was intended as a missionary of the north (to convert the Danes and the rest of the north to Christianity). Though King Horik I claimed he had nothing to do with it, everything points to him being the instigator of this attack.

It is believed that the Frankish-forced conversion of the Saxons could have been one cause of the start of the Viking age in English history. The Danes saw themselves at open war with the Franks and the attacks were perhaps a message to the Anglo-Saxon missionaries, although we cannot say for certain what the motivation of the Danes or the other groups of Norsemen were. Raiding was also a common feature in the sagas when it came to the pre-Viking age – the Viking Age just took it to a new level.

Although a Norse attack on Lindisfarne in AD 793 is commonly identified as the beginning of the 'Viking Age', Norse attacks on Britain did take place prior to this. The 'Viking Age' is, of course, a timeframe set retrospectively to demonstrate some specific events. However, in reality, it was a long-term development of a conflict between the Christianised part of Europe and that of the Pagan Norse. This can be read in *Viking* by Jeanette Varberg, curator of the National Museum of Denmark:

> The attacks of the Vikings did not come out of the blue. They were part of a long conflict between Northern Europe and Western

> Europe, which has its roots in the upheavals of the Migration Period and battles between war kings, each with their own faith (Pagan and Christian). The difference between what we call the Viking Age and the time before was more likely that the attacks increased and not least that the number of written sources, that described Viking attacks, grew extensively from the end of the 8th century onwards.[2]

An entry from the *Anglo-Saxon Chronicle* from AD 787–789 records:

> Here Beorhtric took King Offa's daughter Eadburh. And in his days, there came for the first time three ships; and then the reeve rode there and wanted to compel them to go to the King's town, because he did not know what they were; and they killed him. Those were the first ships of the Danish men which sought out the land of the English race.[3]

This very same event is also mentioned in the Canterbury Manuscript, written in the middle to late eighth century, though here they record that the attackers were from Hordaland but still call them Danish men. The Peterborough Manuscript, a version of the *Anglo-Saxon Chronicle*, calls them Norsemen, although Norsemen does not need to mean Norwegian as many believe. Norsemen is also the word the Franks used for all Vikings, regardless of where they came from. It simply means those coming from the north. The vast majority going to what is today's England and France came from Denmark.

A DNA study of the Viking world conducted in 2020 proved clearly that Danes mainly settled in what is today's England, whereas the Norwegians went to Scotland, the Orkneys and settled in Iceland and Greenland; they also travelled further afield to America, and the Swedes went east.

Danelaw eventually comprised of an area created by a treaty made after the Battle of Edington between a victorious Alfred the Great and the defeated Guthrum, who was baptised into Christianity right after the treaty was signed, taking Alfred as godfather. Guthrum then ruled from York over the area set out in the treaty. Although this area would eventually become known as the Danelaw, Danelaw was not named as a geographical term before the eleventh century.

In this 'Danelaw' area we see, throughout time, elements of folklore deriving from both Danish and pre-Christian beliefs. Of course, they would have been much like the beliefs the Anglo-Saxons imported when arriving in Britain some centuries earlier. However, given the Anglo-Saxons' subsequent conversion to Christianity, many of these beliefs might have been lost. But some of the ideas could have gone back as far as the Roman era of Tacitus.

It is important to be aware that beliefs are not static but change over time, depending on events and time periods; however, at the core there is a set of beliefs that stretch back far in time. Over the centuries, deities and traditions would have varied but the main gods were much the same. Just as water and sacred groves were associated with the transcendence of the Germanic people. Water was considered to be a conduit to the Otherworld or the world of the Gods. Numbers are given importance, with numbers nine and three being a common theme. Then the influence of Celtic culture on the Germanic and vice versa can be seen in various ways, and items recovered in archaeological digs play a huge part in connecting these different cultures. A good example of this is the Gundestrup Cauldron and the Dejbjerg wagons, both examples of Celtic craftmanship that were found in Denmark – which was solely Germanic. Of course, these similarities may have been due to their common Indo-European origin and may simply mean that the cultures were related, especially in areas where they lived as neighbours.

1

Folklore in Daily Life

Today we are often presented with the idea that daily life is separate from religion. For example, many visit church on a Sunday and then go back to their daily routines. By contrast, go back a few hundred years and the lines between folklore, religion and everyday living were far more fluid. Take breadmaking as an example. Today breadmaking sits firmly in the sphere of the daily, non-religious domain. It was not always so. Once the daily baking of bread had rituals attached to it – in the Christian era, for example, crosses were cut into the bread, to protect the breadmaking from various evil powers and from being stolen by Otherworldly beings. Here we see how rituals would once cross over into daily life, and therefore when dealing with the topic of folklore, attempting to make a division between religious and secular spheres of society is not always helpful. This is also true of the pre-Christian era. In a similar way, so-called 'witch marks' were carved or cut into secular buildings to ward off evil. The term 'witch marks' has little to do with witches themselves, but rather the marks functioned to ward of the evil magic associated with witchcraft. However, the marks were not only used to protect people from witches, but they were also used to ward off evil spirits, demons, Otherworldly beings etc. The practice of witch-marking was simply to protect people from harmful magic in general.

In essence, faith, religion, beliefs or rituals and Otherworldly beings were as much a part of daily life as baking bread and cleaning the house. For the ordinary person, there was a need to reach out to gods, or Otherworldly beings, to protect the household from various evils and to gain prosperity. In this there is no difference between the Neolithic period and the Christian era. Simple day-to-day rituals were built in to protect and to assure prosperity. When building a house, the Iron Age man placed a little sacrifice in the post holes to protect the household from various evils. Buried horse skulls under the floor of the house, to ward off evil, were seemingly commonplace until as late as the eighteenth century in Britain, Ireland, Germany and Scandinavia. In some places even further up in time.

Though the Church sometimes sought to eradicate these rituals, the ordinary population continued, with such practices unabated. This ranges from the carving of witch marks on buildings, so that evil could not enter, to the recitation of little rhymes to ensure the safe production of butter and to protect a household from malicious magic aimed at both.

Often, we are presented with the idea that the figures and creatures of folklore consist of simple characters invented from a writer's imagination, but, in reality, we see glimpses of the old pre-Christian beliefs in these symbols. As Claude Lecouteux writes in his book, *The Hidden History of Elves and the Dwarfs*, 'It touches on the beliefs of our ancestors, and because it leads us onto the path of myth, allowing us to glimpse a non-Christian culture that existed parallel to the clerical culture'.[4]

This is exactly what we see when studying collected folklore beliefs: a glimpse of the old beliefs wrapped in a more modern Christian packaging, but still so recognisable.

2

What Lies in a Name?

Before looking at different groups of people and their customs, we should be aware of how such groups typically came to be named. We unfortunately do not know what the Germanic peoples called themselves since they have left no written records. However, groups were often given names by those who encountered them or who were their enemies. Thus, although often described as barbarians, 'Germanic' was often used as a broader term for many tribes across Europe and in Britain. We cannot therefore speak of a singular homogeneous people, but nevertheless, these various tribes, and groups under that umbrella term did possess some similar cultural traditions. Often, we find no codified meaning or distinction involving say, the Germanic peoples. For example, in some English translations of Tacitus's *Germania* and of Caesar's *Conquest of Gaul*, the word 'Germanic' is translated to 'German'. This fluid terminology surrounding the tribes gives some confusion. For clarity, I therefore prefer 'Germanic' as I consider 'German' to be the people living in the modern state of Germany.

In Caesar's *Commentarii de Bello Gallico* (*Conquest of Gaul*) this potential for confusion further becomes apparent:

> When Caesar inquired of them what states were in arms, how powerful they were, and what they could do, in war, he received the following information: that the greater part of the Belgae were descended from the Germans, and that having crossed the Rhine at an early period, they had settled there, on account of the fertility of the country, and had driven out the Gauls who inhabited those regions; and that they were the only people who, in the memory of our fathers, when all Gaul was overrun, had prevented the Teutones and the Cimbri from entering their territories.[5]

As the Germanic tribes that encountered the Romans did not leave much written evidence of themselves, we are left relying on the writings of the Romans and the Christians of Europe. These writings are often coloured by the writers' perspective and agenda such as, for example, where the Germanic people are referred to as 'barbarians'. The name itself is something the Romans gave them. Some of the first descriptions we have of these groups are from Tacitus in *Germania* and Caesar in his *Bello Gallico*. Tacitus was a Roman historian and politician. Caesar conquered Gaul (a Celtic area) as a general in AD 50 and thereby came to the border of 'Germania' and in direct contact with the people inhabiting the area. Since it was the Romans who described the Germanic people and the land they lived in, we need to consider that it would be wrong to simply take the Roman worldview of the Germanic tribes as facts. There were many various tribes with different customs. Tacitus describes them thus:

> The Germanic themselves are, I would say, the original inhabitants of the land and not in the least mixed with those coming from outside – be it by immigration or by visiting guests.[6]

Tacitus speaks from a Greco-Roman cultural outlook where the Germanic people are 'barbarians' and an 'original population', just as Columbus saw the natives of America as a new, original population at a lower stage of evolutionary development.

This viewpoint is further underlined in Strabo's *Geography*:

> Now the parts beyond the Rhenus, immediately after the country of the Celti, slope towards the east and are occupied by the Germans, who though they vary slightly from the Celtic stock in that they are wilder, taller and have yellower hair, are in all respects similar, for in build, habits and modes of life they are such as I have said the Celti are. And I think that it was for this reason that the Romans assigned them the name 'Germani' as they wished to indicate thereby that they were 'Genuine' Galatae, for in the language of the Romans 'Germani' means 'Genuine'.[7]

This illustrates that Tacitus used and commonised a geographical area known as 'Germani' as a term to be used to refer to the inhabitants populating the area.

The Romans (and Greeks) also described these tribes as 'Interpretatio Romana', in essence, imposing their cultural perception and world view onto a system of beliefs of the people outside of their culture. 'Interpretatio Romana',

Latin for 'Roman interpretation', describes the way that the Romans viewed primarily the gods of the Germanic tribes, comparing them to their own deities, but also illustrates how they view the tribes themselves. Therefore, we cannot count on the fact that the gods Tacitus mentions actually compare with the Roman Gods, or that the Germaini, for example, actually had the characteristics that the Romans thought they had.

A Danish author describes the term:

> It is a linguistic and stylistic phenomenon that is important for the understanding of texts in Latin, which were written by Romans and deal with foreign cultures and people. Especially when the description concerns foreign gods.[8]

We are on slightly steadier ground when it comes to customs that bear no resemblance to Roman beliefs. Here we might assume Tacitus is describing actual events observed among the Germanic people. Of course, this information does not come from Tacitus's own experiences and is taken from other people's accounts. Julius Caesar had some direct dealings with this specific group of tribes as a firsthand experience, but his account is also heavily coloured by his political ambitions and Roman world view.

Tacitus also speaks of local customs differing between individual tribes when he gives us a detailed description of the 'Suebi' Swabians. He writes in great detail about a traditional characteristic different from other tribes – the Swabian hair knot. The men traditionally put their hair up in a knot on their heads. He goes on to explain that only freemen wore it like that, and that it distinguished freemen from slaves.[9]

Interestingly, some archaeological finds have confirmed this distinctive hairstyle. The Österby Man was found in a bog just outside Österby, close to Egernførde in South Schleswig in today's Germany, and the Dätgen man was found near Dätgen, south-west of Kiel in Schleswig-Holstein. The Österby Man and the Dätgen Man are both from the Roman period and have been dated between 135 BC and AD 385. It was peat digging that brought the bodies to light in 1948, very similar to the Danish and Irish bog bodies that have been found. When the men were placed in the bog, this area could have belonged to the Angles or the Saxons – their neighbours being the Suebi. In this specific case, archaeology confirms the writing of Tacitus about the hair knot and brings credibility to his writings.

An interesting detail about the Dätgen man was that next to the head a body was later found, pinned down by wooden stakes through the body, which have made scholars speculate that this was a sign of an 'again walker'.

> In 1959, a headless body was discovered by peat cutters in a bog near Dätgen, a village in the district of Rendsburg-Eckernförde in Schleswig-Holstein, Germany. The body was found with four wooden stakes … which scholars have long speculated was indicative of a fear that the body would be ´come a 'wiedergänger' or an 'again walker', a type of undead or restless spirit represented in Germanic folklore. The practice is staking bodies into the bog was not unusual.[10]

This idea of 'again walking' was not uncommon in the Iron Age and Viking Age among the Norse tribes.

So, although accounts of social customs can range from the vague to the detailed and from the understated to the exaggerated, and in all cases cannot be taken as a given, this does not mean that we cannot learn anything from these old sources when it comes to the beliefs of the various tribes. As with all sources, we just need to be aware of who wrote them and why. In some cases, archaeology gives us a helping hand as this noteworthy example has shown us.

As the aim of the book is to explore beliefs and folklore through time, we need an understanding of the beliefs of the Germanic tribes to really understand their viewpoint. Therefore, a critical examination of these very old sources is needed to understand them correctly. This is, of course, not always an easy task – it never is with sources this old – but some understanding of the faith of these elusive tribes is possible. Although we cannot take it for granted that Tacitus and other writers are absolutely truthful in their accounts, or that the names of the gods he mentions in connection with the Germanic people match his Roman perception of them, some understanding of the beliefs of these tribes is possible, especially when archaeology unveils findings that are similar to what is stated in the old sources. Therefore, for the purpose of this book, a view on the sources and what they can tell us about old beliefs are beneficial.

3

Animal and Human Sacrifice

With regards to religion, one aspect that Tacitus and other sources mention is that the Germanic people did not have temples in which to worship their gods, and that they sacrificed humans. When looking at this, it is important to once again remember that many of the beliefs and customs that the Germanic tribes had in common, be they sacred groves, trees, or springs, were all places where they would sacrifice and reach out to the gods.

> At Trelleborg in Denmark, a sacrificial place [a so-called 'horg' or hearg in old English] has been found from the time before the construction of the Viking ring fortress in 980/81. Human and animal skeletons as well as jewelry and tools have been found in five nearly three-meter-deep wells. Of the total of five human victims, there are four smaller children aged 4–7.[11]

A similar site was found at Repton, England, where the Great Heathen Army is believed to have been encamped in AD 873–74. Here four skeletons of children was found next to the burial site of the many Norse graves at the Repton site.

> A chilling truth – which sounds like a cross between a horror movie and an apocalyptic thriller – hides behind a picture of quintessential English calm.
>
> In the quiet shade of trees, children were buried, perhaps to honour hundreds of dead piled nearby.[12]

For many years, doubts surrounded source material that mention human sacrifices. We have several descriptions of human sacrifice, but these are mentioned by people from a different period, who did not witness these events first-hand, as with the two examples. Adam of Bremen, in 1072, describes the sacrifices at Uppsala in Sweden and Thietmar of Merseburg recounts in the eleventh century, how people met every nine years in January at Lejre in Denmark:

> And offer to their gods 99 people and just as many horses, dogs and hens or hawks, for these should serve them in the kingdom of the dead and atone for their evil deeds.[13]

Odin, god of the higher classes and royalty, was thought to require human sacrifices. Both Adam of Bremen and Thietmar of Merseburg wrote centuries after the events and might have been prone to exaggeration. However, put together with other sources and archaeological finds, there seems to be some truth to their statements. Did the Saxons, then, practise this type of sacrifice when they arrived and settled in England? Bede mentions how the Saxons slaughtered or sacrificed cattle:

> And because they have been used to slaughter many oxen in the sacrifices to devils [they may….] celebrate the solemnity with religious feasting, and no more offer beasts to the Devil, but kill cattle to the praise of God in their eating.[14]

Although the account is coloured by the Christian background of Bede, there seems to be some merit to the tale.

The examples of human sacrifice did not come from the Anglo-Saxon period; in fact, no human remains believed to have come from human sacrifices in the Anglo-Saxon period have been found. The Tollund Man, found in a peat bog in Denmark with a noose still around his neck, is likely the most famous find that indicates human sacrifice did occur. Upon his death by strangulation, he was gently put into the bog, his eyes closed and looking like he was sleeping.

With the Tollund Man, the Österby Man, and other such bog bodies, archaeology does seem to confirm the writings of the Romans who stated that the Germanic tribes sacrificed humans. We can also be fairly sure that they are sacrifices from the way that they have been put into the bog and the presence of other sacrificial elements, such as food and other items. It has been argued that if human sacrifices had taken place, Christians or their clerics that had witnessed or had knowledge of it would have strongly condemned it. We cannot say if this was the case, but animal sacrifices are known to have taken place and both written sources and archaeology have found evidence of animal sacrifices. At Yeavering, in Northumberland, a pit filled with animal remains was excavated and dated to the time of the Saxon immigration.[15] The remains were mostly oxen, thus confirming Bede's words on the sacrifice of animals. Of course, this is not proof that the pre-Christian Anglo-Saxons made human sacrifices, as human remains have not been discovered, but it does tell us that the rites of the Angles, Saxons and Jutes were like those of the Germanic tribes described by Tacitus and the later Norsemen of the Viking age.

I have previously mentioned the Österby Man, with the Swabian hair knot, who was discovered in a bog in an area equivalent to where either Angles or Saxons lived. This man had met a violent fate and had been placed in a bog as a sacrifice.

Such a practice has been described among the Saxons. A Gallo-Roman aristocrat and writer, Sidonius Apollinarius, stated in a letter in the fifth century:

> Moreover, when the Saxons are setting sail from the continent, and are about to drag their firm-holding anchors from an enemy's shore, it is their usage, thus homeward bound, to abandon every tenth captive to the slow agony of a watery end, casting lots with perfect equity among the doomed crowd in execution of this iniquitous sentence of death. This custom is all the more deplorable in that it is prompted by honest superstition. These men are bound by vows which have to be paid in victims, they conceive it a religious act to perpetrate this horrible slaughter, and to take anguish from the prisoner in place of ransom; this polluting sacrilege is in their eyes an absolving sacrifice.[16]

We cannot prove the Saxons sacrificed people to the ocean, since we have no remains left. We can, however, see that a violent end was met by the Österby Man, the Dätger Man and the Tollund Man and the rites sound similar to that mentioned by Tacitus and what is described about the Norsemen by later sources. Archaeological findings, whilst in themselves not definitive proof, do point to the sources being correct. We will likely never know if or by how much these sources exaggerated events or if at all, but some parts of their descriptions do seem to be based on facts. Though no human sacrificial remains have so far been found in England from the Anglo-Saxon Pagan period, thus leaving us with an absence of proof, the written accounts and archaeology from other areas of Europe point to such rituals having happened. As we have been told by Adam of Bremen and Thietmar of Merseburg, some of these human sacrifices were hung in tree groves. In these cases, for the most part, the residue of those sacrificed would have decomposed after being exposed to the weather. The special chemical conditions, namely acidic and oxygen-poor water in raised bogs, are the reason for the preservation of the so-called bog bodies. The same conditions are not present when it comes to bodies exposed to the weather above ground. This means that in most instances, if both human and animal sacrifices occurred, their remains would most likely have decomposed and for that very reason will never been found.

The most we can say for certain is that the Anglo-Saxons certainly sacrificed animals to their gods, a practice similar to later arrivals such as the Vikings. That the Anglo-Saxons had similar traditions as those of the Vikings is also proven by a grave from Bidford-on-Avon. In his book *The Viking Way,* Neil Price believes that the person buried here was a cunning woman. She was buried with an array of unusual items such as scalpels, antler cones, metal cylinders, and items considered amulets all contained in a leather bag. This points to her being a healer and having a special status in life.[17]

Burials of this kind, with perceived magical items, are found across the whole of the Scandinavian area. Many of these graves in Scandinavia dating from the Viking Age contain a staff considered to be a symbol of the Völva, the seeress of the Viking world. Völva means staff bearer and the description in the sagas are very similar to that of finds from the archaeological world.

4

Pagan 'Holy' Places

As Tacitus stated in his *Germania,* completed around AD 98, the Germanic tribes did not worship in temples but in groves and nature, and we do have accounts of how and where the Germanic tribes worshipped their gods.

> They conceive it unworthy of the grandeur of celestial beings to confine their deities within walls, or to represent them under a human similitude: Wood and groves are their temples; and they affix names of divinity to that secret power, which they behold with the eye of adoration alone.[18]

But can we believe these reports? No temples from this early timeframe have been found in archaeology although research into place names does seem to show that there were groves and places that were sacred

Trees and Groves as Holy Places

One of the most prominent trees in myth is of course the great tree of Yggdrasil, the giant ash tree that carries the nine worlds in Norse and Germanic beliefs. The first man was understood to be made from an ash tree (Ask, who it is presumed, although not explicitly stated, that he was made from Yggdrasil itself), and the first woman, Embla, from an elm tree, underlining the importance of trees in the myths of Scandinavia. Yggdrasil means the 'terrible' or 'Odin's horse', and many Scandinavian royals believed themselves descendants of Odin. The elm tree, which women are made from, is also believed to have healing properties and is connected to the elves. Coming from a similar geographical area to the Norse/Vikings, the Anglo-Saxons would have believed similar myths when they arrived on the shores of Britain.

In pre-Christian beliefs, trees had spirits or personalities of their own, an in-dwelling being if you will. The trees were integral parts of the Cosmos, connecting the home of the gods to that of humans and ultimately to the roots of the Underworld.

This can be read in the *Younger Edda*, in *Gylfaginning*.

> By the ashes of Yggdrasil, there the Gods hold their judgments every day. The ash is the largest and best of all trees. Its branches spread over the whole world and stand above the sky. Three roots hold the tree up and stand immeasurably wide.[19]

Yggdrasil carries the Nine worlds: Niflheim, the world of fog; Muspelheim, the world of fire; Asgard, the world of the gods; Midgard, the world of men; Jötunheim, home of the giants; Vanaheim, home of the Vanir; Álfheim, the realm of the elves, a beautiful, light world; Svartálfheim, home of the dwarfs; and Helheim, home of the dead for those who died of natural causes. The tree teems with various animals, including creatures ranging from deer to scary serpents. Ratatosk is the squirrel connecting and bringing messages from the eagle at the top to the serpent or dragons at the foot of the tree. The name Ratatosk means something like drill-tooth or bore-tooth.

Other sources also mention sacred groves and trees. According to the eighth-century *Vita Bonifatii auctore Willibaldo*, the Anglo-Saxon missionary Bonifatius, with his retinue, felled a tree for this purpose around the year AD 724.

> Now many of the Hessians who at that time had acknowledged the Catholic faith were confirmed by the grace of the Holy Spirit and received by the grace of the Holy Spirit and received the laying-on of hands. But others, not as strong in the spirit, refused to accept the pure teaching of the church in their entirety. Moreover, some continued secretly, others openly, to offer sacrifices to trees and springs, to inspect the entrails of victims; some practiced divination, legerdemain, and incantations; some turned their attention to auguries, auspices, and other sacrificial rites; while others, of a more reasonable character, forsook all the profane practices of the gentiles [i.e., Pagans] and committed none of these crimes. With the counsel and advice of the latter persons, Boniface in their presence attempted to cut down at a place called Gaesmere, a certain oak of extraordinary size called in the old tongue of the pagans the Oak of Jupiter.[20]

Jupiter is the same god as Thor, or Donar. Thor was a sky god, the god who, with his powers, created rain and fertility, as well as thunder and lightning. In the Viking Age he was a more common and popular god than Odin. A tree or pillar of similar importance to the Saxons was cut down by the forces of Charlemagne at the beginning of the Saxon wars. The royal Frankish annals have an entry for AD 772:

> The most gracious lord King Charles then held an assembly at Worms. From Worms he marched first into Saxony, capturing the castle at Eresburg, he proceeded as far as the Irminsul, destroyed this Idol and carried away the gold and silver which he found.[21]

In old Saxon 'Irminsul' means something like the great pillar. Rudulf of Fulda describes a similar 'Universal Column, upholding all things'; it appears it was a tree trunk or pillar of some sort placed in nature to worship. Later sources such as Adam of Bremen and Thietmar of Merseburg state the same thing and it was in these sacred groves, as mentioned in the previous chapter, that various sacrifices appear to have been hung from trees.

In place names we can also find indications of these Germanic Pagan practices. In Danish place names such as Thorslund and Frølund we have evidence of these groves and trees. Scandinavian place names are often constructed with words such as Lundr (grove), or viðr (tree) combined with the names of gods. A good example of such is Onsholt near Aarhus, which consist of Odin and holt or Odin's Forest. Odense comes from two compound words Odin and Vi, meaning a sacrificial grove. This means that the city of Odense was once a Pagan cult centre where Odin was worshipped. Archaeology excavations have also revealed formed soil layers in an area north of the Nonnebakken (Viking ring fortress) which may have been a hǫrgr, (in old Norse, 'hearg' in old English)[22] – a traditional altar or cult site consisting of a heap of stones. These horgh/heargs indicate that these rites took place outside in nature.

Similar place names are found in England. As an example, the village of Grimscote means Grim's Cott – Grim being another name for Woden (or Odin). Harrow, London, comes from the old English word 'Hearg' – as mentioned an altar or place of worship outside in nature. Other examples are Wanborough (meaning Woden's Barrow), Wensley (Woden's Meadow) and Wormshill (deriving from Woden's Hill). Also, in Harrow is Grim's Ditch, also known as Grimsdyke, a section of Anglo-Saxon trenches. Grim's Ditch (Hampshire) is another set of earthworks, while Grim's Ditch (South Oxfordshire) are Iron Age/early Roman-era earthworks.

The examples are many and these place names can be found not just in Britain and Scandinavia but across Europe in the areas where the Germanic people lived. These place names show clearly that the Anglo-Saxons had the same beliefs and worshipped in the same places as those of the later arrivals, the Vikings. If we put this together with the old sources, we do gain a picture of Anglo-Saxons worshipping the same gods in the same places as those of the continental Germanic tribes and the later Vikings.

5

Water as a Gateway to the Transcendent

There is no doubt that water was truly central to the imaginary world surrounding the gods and the transcendent.

Tacitus recounts these sacrificial groves in a paragraph on the Longobardi, who have genetically been linked to Scandinavia. They were one of the barbarian groups invading Italy in the migration period. We are told of the goddess Nethus, who was drawn around the country on a chariot:

> In an Island of the ocean stands a sacred and unviolated grove, in which is a consecrated chariot, covered with a veil, which the priest alone is permitted to touch. He becomes conscious of the entrance of the goddess into this secret recess; and with profound veneration attends the vehicle, which is drawn by yoked cows. At this season all is joy; and every place which the goddess deigns to visit is a scene of festivity. No wars are undertaken; arms are untouched; very hostile weapons are kept away. Peace abroad and at home are then only known.[23]

Do we perhaps encounter a somewhat garbled tale of the above in the story about King Frode Fredegod III in *Gesta Danorum* by Saxo Grammaticus? Saxo Grammaticus was a Danish monk who wrote *Gesta Danorum: History of the Danes* towards the end of the twelfth century and the beginning of the thirteenth. He collected and told stories from the Danish past, and included among those the legends of the Scyldings, the Danish royal house, mentioned in Beowulf. King Frode's reign, according to Saxo and Sturluson's *Younger Edda*, was around the time of Christ.

According to the story, when King Frode died, he was taken around the country on a cart and placed within so that people would think he was still alive. It has been suggested that people believed he was the god Frey himself, the god who brings peace and prosperity to the country. During this king's reign, peace was so extensive that people spoke of the 'Frodefred' – Peace of Frode. This very description of King Frode is very similar to the description about the chariot from Tacitus. It becomes even more interesting when you look at archaeological finds.

The Dejbjerg wagons were taken apart and laid down in a bog in West Jutland, Denmark, around 100 BC. In a description from the Danish National Museum, we are told:

> From this period come the Wagons from Dejbjerg, which were sacrificed in a west Jutland bog just before the Birth of Christ. They were dismantled and laid in a peat bog, fenced in with branches and wattles. The Wagons from Dejbjerg were probably the ceremonial carriages of a magnate. The iron in the carriage bodies was forged from continental mountain ore, and the carriages were probably made in central Europe by Celtic artisans. However, the wheels were repaired in Denmark; one of the rim hoops was forged from Danish bog iron ore.[24]

Six of these chariots have been found in Denmark, of which the two from Dejbjerg are the most famous. During this period the Jutes and the Angles had not yet immigrated to what was to become England, so they would have inhabited this area where the wagons were found, although the culture of the Danish tribes would not have been much different. Of course, Tacitus's description cannot be taken as complete fact, nor would he have known the diversity of customs among the various tribes, but it is striking that he describes this rite with a chariot when we have found such chariots laid down in bogs as sacrifices.

Tacitus also explains to us what happened to the chariot after it had been dragged around the kingdom:

> The chariot, with its curtain, and, if we may believe it, the goddess herself, then undergo ablution in a secret lake. This office is performed by slaves, whom the same lake instantly swallows up. Hence proceeds a mysterious horror; and a holy ignorance of what that can be, which is beheld only by those who are about to perish.[25]

The lake here was seen as a gateway to the Otherworld, and there are many more examples of water being considered an approach to the divine. One such example is the wooden man from Rude Eskildstrup. This was a form of god image found in a bog and is one of several such finds. Additionally, many of the bog finds were likely both human and animal sacrifices, and interestingly they are found alongside weapons.

Of the human victims, the Tollund Man is probably the most noteworthy and famous; he was sacrificed between the year 405–384 BC. Tissø, a sacred lake, where offerings were made is another good example from Denmark. All this illustrates that lakes and waterways were considered liminal spaces – a place from which you could reach the Otherworld or the gods.

As demonstrated by both the Tollund Man and the Österby Man, bogs were a chosen place for sacrifice. The same can be said for lakes and rivers. The river valley at Illerup Ådal and the wetlands at Alkens Enge in Denmark revealed interesting archaeological finds that match what sources tell us about sacrifices, including humans, and the use of water as a conduit. Here, at Illerup Ådal, large quantities of weapons were deposited in the years between AD 200–450, and Alkens Enge has revealed human sacrifices dating from around the year AD 1. Here it is believed that an entire army was sacrificed after a fierce battle took place in central Jutland, between a local army and a force from outside. Though not necessarily connected to a Roman army, Illerup Ådal also revealed the largest amount of sacrificed Roman weapons ever found in Denmark. The personal items, such as combs, point to the army coming from what is today's Norway.

Another interesting aspect of water myths is the use of wells as both a place of sacrifice and a way of gaining knowledge. In *Gylfaginning* (the fooling of Gylfe) by Snorri Sturluson, we find the story of Mimir's Well. We are told that Odin sacrifices his one eye to be allowed to drink from the well – this supposedly gives him knowledge and wisdom:

> stand wide apart; one root is with the Aesir's and another with the frost-giants, where Ginungagap formerly was; the third reaches into Niflheim; under it is Hvergelmer, where Nidhug gnaws at the root from below. But under the second root, which extends to the frost giants, is the well of Mimer, wherein knowledge and wisdom are concealed. The owner of the well, high Mimer. He is full of wisdom, for he drinks from the well with the Gjallar-horn.[26]

Nidhogg (Nidhug) is one of the many serpents of the Norse myth living below Yggdrasil and gnawing at its roots. Odin revives Mimir's head with runes and a galdr, so he can talk to Mimir, thus gaining the knowledge Mimir obtained from the well water.

Water from another well keeps Yggdrasil alive. Yggdrasil is the mythical ash tree at the centre of the Norse Cosmos, connecting the nine worlds – including Asgard, Midgard, and Helheim – as the 'Tree of Life'.

Below Yggdrasil's roots was the well of Urdr. This was the well of destiny, named after one of the Norns who determined the destiny of gods and humans alike. Norns are beings in the Norse Cosmos who control fate. Watering Yggdrasil from the well daily, the Norns nourished it, keeping it vibrant and the nine worlds alive. The best known of the several Norns are the three primary Norns – Urðr (Wyrd), Verðandi, and Skuld. These three names usually translate to past, present and future.

Wells also played a significant role in the human world. Once again, we can connect the information we gain from the old sources with the material world. Trees, groves, and wells are central, both as places of sacrifice (proven by archaeology) and in myths. The symbolism in using a well for a sacrifice makes sense, considering the importance the wells of both Mimir and Urdr have in the myth.

6

Animism

The pre-Christian faith of the Norsemen, Vikings and the Celts all believed in the idea of animism, a belief system that everything in nature had a spirit. Stones, trees, rivers, and other natural features were alive, and were understood to have their own spirits or personalities and therefore were considered sacred. We still find similar notions of this in folklore across Europe.

A prime example of an animistic being in the minds of people is the Elder Mother, said to live in the elder tree in Denmark according to folklore of a rather recent date, as these were stories told in the nineteenth century. However, if we go back even earlier, we can posit a connection to the pre-Christian era. Some researchers suggest the Elder Mother was originally the Goddess Freya. You had to ask her for permission if you wanted to cut down an elderberry or cut branches from it as the elder tree was the Mother's property. There was also a ritual to be followed: to be allowed to take anything from the tree, you had to walk backwards away from the tree and say three times:

> 'Elder mother, Elder mother, Elder mother, give me some of your tree and I will give you some of mine'.

Only then could you cut branches off the tree or cut it down. If you forgot to perform this ritual, it meant misfortune and death amongst your livestock. In the worst case, you called down your own death by cutting down an elder bush. Furthermore, we find belief in the concept of fairy entities as elves were also associated with the elder tree. In a kind of circularity or continuum, as is often the case, folklore is a somehow a seamless mix of various beliefs and stories. The elves, or in Danish 'ellefolk', are associated with the god Frey, as he was the Lord of Álfheim, the realm of the elves, while the Elder Mother has been associated with the goddess Freya, his sister. We will return to Álfheim later.

7

The Völva

As far as we can tell from Viking Age Tales, the Germanic tribes had the Völva – the seeress – who governed their spiritual practices. These women are described in the Norse and Viking sagas and we also have information from Tacitus pointing to the existence of such women. According to Tacitus, the Germanic people believed their women contained holy psychic powers:

> They even suppose somewhat of sanctity and prescience to be inherent in the female sex; and therefore, neither despise their counsels, nor disregard their responses.[27]

Tacitus also describes an ancient Germanic practice of divination, the likes of which may have been performed by a seeress:

> No people are more addicted to divination by omens and lots. The latter is performed in the following simple manner. They cut a twig from a fruit-tree, and divide it into small pieces, which distinguished by certain marks, are thrown promiscuously upon a white garment.[28]

It has been suggested that this is the first description of runic sticks – but this cannot be confirmed or proven. At Blidegn, on Funen Island in Denmark, a grave from the first century AD has been found, containing what is believed to be high-status woman. Many of the artefacts were believed to have magical properties such as petrified sea urchins, some odd-shaped stones which showed signs of use of some kind, and a bundle of about ten twigs which was found partially wrapped in thread made of wool. The contents of the grave point to the woman being a sorceress. Tacitus mentions lot taking and tell us how they took twigs from a fresh sapling and carved some sticks which they used for divination. So here we have the description from Tacitus which seems to be confirmed by the finding of a woman's grave, the contents pointing to her as a possible divinatory seeress, just as we have similar archaeological findings from the Bronze Age containing twigs. At the time of the Bronze Age it seems that both men and women could be cult specialists, whereas later the characteristics of a seer are to be found mainly in women from the Iron Age onwards.

Other graves have also been found which are believed to contain the remains of Norse seeresses, and objects have been recovered that are very similar to the attire and equipment described in the sagas, including spears and staff-like objects. Around forty to fifty of these graves have been found around Scandinavia, some of them considered deviant burials. The most famous ones are perhaps the Oseberg ship burial in Norway, a ninth-century Viking ship containing the remains of two high-status women, and the grave of the suspected Völva found at Fyrkat, one of the ring fortresses of Harald Bluetooth in Denmark, who, it is believed, may have been a Pagan sorceress and advisor to Harald. The Fyrkat remains are certainly a high-status woman whose grave objects included a metal staff and seeds from the poisonous henbane plant, both objects associated with a sorceress.

Henbane (*Hyoscyamus niger*), often called the 'Witch's Herb', was a primary ingredient in historical 'witch's salves' or 'flying ointments' during the Middle Ages and early modern period. The plant was highly hallucinogenic and gave the feeling of flying. It was believed that this drug helped the Völva gain knowledge, giving her the ability to see things others could not. The drug might have assisted her in evoking the trance-like state needed for seidr, a form of magic discussed in more detail in the next chapter.

In the *Laxdæla Saga*, a staff is literally called a seidr staff. The *Laxdæla Saga* is an Icelandic saga about 'the people of Lax Ådalen'. The saga is one of the four best-known and most extensive, with a huge gallery of characters.

> In the ground below were some bluish-black and hideous bones, a buckle, and a large magic wand. People concluded from this that it was a Völva's grave. The bones were taken to a secluded place far from the usual paths of men.[29]

Another grave from Denmark, at Trekroner Grydehøj, contains a high-status woman buried with similar content, including a staff-like object made of bronze and iron, believed to be a Völva's staff. Besides the staff, the grave contained two women, half a man, a horse, a dog cut in half, a small bauta stone and large boulders. Unlike equestrian graves, the grave contained no riding gear (the horse is interpreted as an animal able to take the deceased person to the other world). As we shall see later, horses are seen as animals which can move between worlds, thus making this animal part of the burial rites to accompany the dead to the world of spirits. Horses in graves are usually connected to high-status burials as they were both a status symbol and also connected to Odin and the horses of other gods. Large boulders were thrown in over the deceased and the deposited grave goods placed at the end of the grave.

Another grave from the ninth century also worth mentioning can be found at Gerdrup (north of Roskilde) in Denmark. This grave bears similarities with the grave from Trekroner Grydehøj, because it has large boulders placed on top of the deceased person. This can be read from Roskilde Museum:

> Two graves appeared under the soil. One, grave A, was just a small hole with the remains of a cremated human. The other, grave B was larger and turned out to be a burial grave with two human skeletons side by side. The skeletons were well-preserved enough that the sex and approximate age could be determined. One was from a man of 35–40, who was lying on his back with his ankles crossed, and his head twisted unnaturally down towards his left shoulder. This indicated that he had been bound at the ankles and had been hanged before the burial. The other skeleton was that of a middle-aged woman, also laid on her back and weighed down by large stones. At her belt was a small needle case, and near her right shin an iron lance point. Based on the shape of the lance, the archaeologists were able to date the grave to the 9th century, that is, the Viking Age.[30]

Many of these graves that are believed to belong to Völvas are high-status graves and often contain imported goods of various kinds, although this is not always the case. What we can learn from the burials is that the Völvas or staff bearers were both highly respected but also in some cases feared. An interesting aspect of the Trekroner Grydehøj and the Gerdrup graves are indeed the large boulders placed on top of the deceased. These findings correlate with what we are told in the sagas about people who were accused of malign magic.

In the *Laxdæla Saga*, we find a story of a family believed to be skilled in witchcraft. They are accused of malign sorcery and of killing a boy with their galdr. (A galdr is a magical enchantment, in this case malign magic, which ends the boy's life.)

> Olaf ordered that Kotkel with his wife and sons should be killed immediately. It was, he said, already far too late. Olaf and Hrut set off with fifteen men. But when Kotkel saw them coming on horseback, he fled with his family up into the mountains. There the son Halbjorn Grindstone Eye was seized, and a skin bag was thrown over his head. Some men were set to watch over him, while the others continued the hunt for Kotkel, Grima and Stigande. The parents were seized on the ridge between Haukadal and Laksaadal, and both were stoned to death, after which they were buried under a stone cairn, which is called Trolledyssen.[31]

The parents are stoned to death and then buried under a stone cairn. This looks very similar to what we find in the Gerdrup and the Trekroner Grydehøj graves. DNA testing of the Gerdrup burial has shown that the grave contains a mother and son. The mother was buried with a staff and a large boulder placed on top of her. Her son was likely hanged and then thrown into the grave. The large boulders suggest that people might have feared she would rise from the grave. It is believed the large boulders were to keep them from returning to haunt the living. The Gerdrup grave makes it even more plausible that this was a Völva or one skilled in sorcery, who was feared. This is suggested due to the deviant burial with large boulders and the items in the grave believed to be an insignia of the status of the deceased.

The bag thrown over the head of the son in the story from the saga points to the belief of the evil eye. The belief was that the deceased could harm them with sorcery if they could see.

Very similar to that from the *Laxdæla Saga* is the story from the *Eyrbyggja Saga* about Katla. In the *Eyrbyggja Saga*, Katla is stoned to death and the man is hung; the grave at Gerdrup shows a similar scenario in which the woman is buried under large boulders, and her son is hung and buried with her. The archaeologist, Leszek Gardela, has therefore suggested that the large stones on top of the deceased along with the spear could be an indicator that the grave contained a cult specialist and that her surroundings showed fear that she would rise from the grave, thus being buried in a similar way as the body from the Dätgen bog.

In Scandinavia, the Völva is known about through the literature of the sagas and most prominently from *The Völuspa*, the best-known poem of the *Poetic Edda*, where Odin seeks a prophecy from the Völva. In the medieval period and after the conversion to Christianity in Denmark, the Völva became known as an evil witch. The Völva's helping spirits slowly turned into the familiars of the witch, purportedly sent to assist by the Devil, and the galdr, a spell or incantation, became forbidden by the Church and the authorities.

However, within the ordinary and secular population as well as within the richer and more informed part of the population, the distinction between malign and benevolent magic continued. Wise women and men were weapons against malign sorcery and the evil-doing witch. Magic or sorcery was considered a tool by which you could achieve various goals, and like all tools, it could be used for both good and evil. Their advice could range from herbs and cough syrup to counselling, from countering various types of evil sorcery to finding out if your child had been replaced by a changeling. As Christianity became more widespread, the Völva's importance diminished and those women who considered themselves thus were pushed to the margins of society. Here they still had their function in society but in a far more withdrawn position. This activity was still looked at with respect but also fear.

8
Seidr

Seidr was a form of magic which could reshape the future. This involved a transformation for the soul, to be able to make the journey to other plains of existence, and through that being able to foretell and reshape the future. This was one kind of magic the Völva was expected to perform.

Both Odin and Freya were masters of seidr. Both are also known to be able to shapeshift. Freya owned a falcon '*hamr*' (garment), allowing her to transform into a falcon, and with Odin, it relates to his shaman-like function and thus being able to travel in all worlds. Odin is the god of wisdom, ecstasy, magic, runes, poetry, and war. As we can see with both the Nordic poem, 'Bjarkemál' and in the story of Kveldulf, who was a shapeshifter and berserker mentioned in the sagas, the trance or sleep is an important part of shapeshifting; by entering a trance one could take a spiritual journey to another world. Kveldulf is the main character in the beginning of *Egil's Saga*. Here it was said of him that when it became close to evening, he changed character. It was said that he was Ulfhednar, meaning he could transform into a wolf, hence the name Kveldulf meaning Evening Wolf.

In a *seidr* ritual, the person involved went into a trance and thereby took a spiritual journey to another world. *Seidr* rituals have great similarities with shamanism, where the journey to other planes also took place by going into a trance.

Kristina Jennbert suggests that the performing of seidr may be representative of the shapeshifting of a person or perhaps even their transformation into the form of the Fylgja, guardian spirits that take the shape of an animal (see Chapter 10), to guide a person on their journey to the realm of the dead. It has been suggested that animal motifs and helping spirits/animals have a great significance for communication with the other world – just as the gods could reach the world of men by changing shape into animals. Perhaps then this trance-like state is, in the seidr, a way by which one can reach the transcendent.

The Norns of the Norse, three powerful female fate goddesses in Norse mythology, were believed to have woven the life thread of all men. This notion of a pre-destiny or fate led Norsemen to believe that their death was pre-determined. Seidr, it was thought, could change this course of fate, both in terms of personal outcomes, but also for larger events like battles, where potentially the fate of many would be death. The Völva was the seeress or witch who could perform these rites, as well as foretell the future; by using seidr and galdr they could essentially change the course of fate.

According to Neil Price, there were seidr for both good and ill, for protection and to do harm:

> There were seiðr rituals for divination and clairvoyance; for seeking out the hidden, both in the secrets of the mind and in physical locations; for healing the sick; for bringing good luck; for controlling the weather; for calling game animals and fish. Importantly, it could also be used for the opposite of these things – to curse an individual or an enterprise; to blight the land and make it barren; to induce illness; to tell false futures and thus to set their recipients on a road to disaster; to injure, maim and kill, in domestic disputes and especially in battle.[32]

The Völva travelled from place to place and performed various acts of magic, galdr and seidr. Freya was the one who taught Odin seidr, thus giving Odin the connection to shamanism and shapeshifting. It has been pointed out that only women are normally allowed to do seidr, making the men 'ergi' (unmanly); however, Odin himself performs seidr and is skilled in sorcery. This claim is based on a single source, so we do not know if this is the correct interpretation.

In the sagas we still hear of men performing magic and thereby, as believed, becoming ergi, but perhaps the case was not as clear cut. As we know the sagas were written down many centuries after the Völva. We do not know how much of the world view really came down to us from the Christian beliefs of the writer. Archaeology tells us that in the case of the Viking Age, evidence was not as clear cut as we would like to be. To take an example, below is a description of a deviant burial from near Lejre, at Roskilde in Denmark. The buried person was a male, but the grave contents held some items which normally would be deemed female. In the sagas and various sources that report on the Viking Age, the cult specialists are usually female.

> Another grave that stood out was A2066, which contained several antiquities scattered in the fill and at the bottom of the grave. It was a fairly large fill of 251 x 208 cm, in which a man was buried.

> Among other things, three knives and two weights were found near the skeleton. What was remarkable was the filling process, where burnt bones were added together with shards of pottery. High in the fill was found, among other things, glass beads, a small bowl-shaped fibula without a needle and a quarter-penny weight, as well as several short iron nails, a coffin hinge and two petrified sea urchins. The majority of the antiquities were thus not found near the skeleton but distributed in the upper 50 cm of the grave's fill. Furthermore, it is striking that while the skeleton is anthropologically assessed to be that of a man, several of the antiquities are of types traditionally associated with women.[33]

The grave content is also of interest, particularly the two petrified sea urchins that were found. Petrified sea urchins are believed to have magical properties. They were used as amulets as far back as the Megalithic period and we find them in the Iron Age and Viking Age in graves believed to contain cult specialists. In 'The Lokasenna' in *The Poetic Edda*, Loki condemns such magic as unmanly knowledge and accuses Odin or performing seidr; unmanly is not a term you would usually associate with Viking Age men. However, we are told that Odin is the master of seidr. Does this grave indicate that men did perform in this area of society? We have a grave which is deviant compared to others and it contains items which have magical properties. At the very least it tells us that we cannot decide the gender of the grave occupant by content alone. From the Viking Age in particular there are more of these graves where the content is less obvious than we would like it to be.

9

Galdr, Runes, Sorcery, and Swords

Saxo, a twelfth-century Danish monk, mentions sorcery in his own words:

> As I occasionally come to talk about such beings and their enterprises, and I do not want the reputation of publishing anything seemingly truthful that goes against the truth or common folk belief, I consider it worthwhile here to tell that in the old days there were three different kinds of miscreants who performed many strange miracles and magic.[34]

Saxo says this in connection with his telling the story of the Danes in *Gesta Danorum*; there is no doubt that sorcery was believed to exist and could be used.

> *Gesta Danorum: History of the Danes.*
> *In the story of Halfdan and Harald. (Both Kings from the Scyldinge line.)*
>
> When Frode died, Halfdan ruled Denmark for about three years; he then handed over the dominion to his brother Harald as deputy and ravaged as a Viking with violence and power the islands and the nearby islands, which are separated from the mainland of Sweden by a curved strait. Here he pulled his ships ashore in the winter and surrounded them with a rampart, and he spent three years on this voyage. He then attacked Sweden and felled the king in one battle. Then he wanted to take up a duel with the king's son Erik, a son of his uncle Frode, and when he had learned that Erik's giant warrior Hake was good at dulling swords with galdr songs, he prepared to strike with a huge club studded

> with iron studs, as if he wanted to overcome the power of sorcery with the power of the tree. Then he – for he surpassed all others by his excellent bravery – in the midst of the fiercest attacks of the enemies, put the helmet on his head, threw the shield and swung the club with both hands against the wall of shields that was raised against him, and no obstacle was so strong, that it was not beaten to bits and pieces by its mighty blow; also the giant, who rushed forward to fight with him, he felled with a fierce blow with his weapon.[35]

A galdr song is sorcery, consisting of a chant or incantations. Seidr is built on the notion that the human mind, in whole or in parts, can interact with forces outside of the body. In this case, the sword was dulled by a galdr, i.e., it becomes blunt and useless, so, the opponent's sword could not harm.

The notion was that you could enchant a sword and give it more power by using magic, chants and spells and by inscribing runes. In this way, you could win victories on the battlefield. At the same time, with such an amulet or a counter-spell, you could effectively block that kind of sorcery. We cannot know whether Halfdan used the power of the tree to counteract the sorcery as Saxo here suggests, but certain types of wood and runes were mentioned as a defence against sorcery. One of the trees known in folklore to have magical properties is hazel, and it was precisely this one that was used when making a 'Nid' pole. Nid or nïo, means to mock or taunt. And a 'Nidding' is a person with no honour.

> Then Egil Skallagrimsson went up to the island, took a hazel pole, went up a slope facing the land, put a horse's head on the end of the pole, read over it and said, 'Here I set up a hazel pole and turned the curse on King Erik and Queen Gunhild'. Then he thrust the rod into the ground and carved runes on it to reveal what curse was placed in it.[36]

He read over it, in other words means he uttered a spell (galdr). The hazel was believed to have magical properties and could also protect against lightning strikes. As with other objects with magical properties, it could be used for both good and evil. Saxo also mentions the 'Nid' pole in his work *Gesta Danorum: History of the Danes*.

In Denmark a little knife was found near Odense in a grave. On the knife runes were edged into it. The knife is dated to around AD 150 making it one of two of the oldest runic inscriptions ever found in Denmark. The inscription itself consists of five runes, ending with three depressions. The text is interpreted as the word 'hirila', which in Old Norse can mean 'Little Sword'. The find was made public in January 2024.

Lead amulets are also found in Denmark which are supposed to protect the person from malign magic, elves and demons. These lead amulets are usually from the medieval era. Lead amulets with runes are small, folded lead plates from the Middle Ages, often containing magical spells or prayers written in runes, although the text is often in Latin. They served as protection against demons, elves or disease and are frequent finds during metal detector searches. About fifty have been found in Denmark.

Further, there are stories about swords from the sagas and the *Gesta Danorum*, some of which have similarities to the legends of King Arthur and Excalibur. In the story of Tyrfing, it is the dwarves who have forged the sword and at the same time put a curse on it as revenge.

> There was a king called Svafrlame; He was a descendant of Odin. Once when he was out hunting, he became separated from his men, and at sunset he passed by a rock where two dwarves were sitting outside. Before they became aware of the king, he had swung a sword with runes on it over them so that they could not slip back into their stones. The king asked them what their names were; One called himself Dvalin and the other Dulin, and both amicably begged for their lives. 'I will give Dvalin and Dulin their lives', said the king, 'if you promise to forge me a sword as good as your genius is capable of; its hilt shall be of gold, and I require it to bite through iron as well as through cloth and never rust. Victory shall follow it, whoever wears it'. The dwarves had no choice and agreed to everything the king demanded, and before he rode away, he set a deadline as to when he would come and retrieve the sword. At the appointed time he rode to the dwarven rock, and when he came forward the dwarves were already standing outside and handed him the sword; As soon as the king had seized it, they ran into the stone, but when Dvalin stood in the door, He turned and said; 'That sword becomes a man's bane every time it is drawn; with that, 3 niddings work will be performed and you will also get your own death from it'. When the king heard Dvalin's words, he slashed at him with his sword, but at the same time the dwarves jumped right into the

> rock, and the door closed behind them; The sword hit nothing but stones, but it sunk so deep into the rock that the blade was hidden on both sides. Svafrlame called his new sword Tyrfing, it shone like a ray in the dark when it was drawn and would not be sheathed until it was reddened with human blood; So bitingly sharp was it that those who were wounded never lived through the day. The king then wore it in many battles, and in all of them he was victorious.[37]

The king swung a sword with runes on it, thus preventing the dwarves from escaping. Firstly, iron was a material that prevents sorcery from working – thus, when you want to protect your child from the sorcery of Otherworldly beings, you can place pins or scissors made of iron or steel in the crib of the baby for protection (more on that later). At the same time, runes make this spell stronger. The sword can cut through the rock because it has been made by the dwarfs, thus being very sharp and having magical properties (dwarfs are thought to be dark elves and are named as master smiths). The gods possess several magical items made by the dwarfs such as Odin's ring, Draupnir. The knowledge of runes is also connected to people skilled in sorcery, and Svafrlame would not have been able to catch the dwarfs outside the rock without some knowledge of runes. Perhaps knowledge in runes and skills in sorcery comes hand in hand. That is at least what we seem to be told, for instance in *The Hávámál* and *The Völuspa* from the *Poetic Edda*.

Another example of runes engraved on a sword is in the story of Hading in the first part of the *Gesta Danorum*:

> You shouldn't, Glavind [Glavind is the sword]
> benefit you, Troll,
> even if you Rune
> have toasted it.
> Witchcraft
> no Heroes subdue;
> believe me, fool,
> Trolls can be tamed.
> Not your Galder
> I dread,
> your life you must let,
> dreadful Giant.
> Not my sword

with Deceit you deafen,
your ugly body
I will cleave.[38]

Here, runes and sorcery are directly connected and in the next verse it says, 'I do not fear your galdr'. We are told in the *Gesta Danorum* that galdr and runes give extra power to the swords or dull the blade of the opponent.

Saxo himself writes that he relates the stories as they were told, but yet again we must be careful with the sources. Though Saxo is from a Danish noble family and must have heard these stories from childhood, he was also a learned monk and had been educated in Europe. Writing the history of the Danes was also a job he received from Absalon, the Danish archbishop at the time, and the purpose was to legitimise the-then current Danish royal line.

Although his storytelling was clearly coloured by his beliefs, excess exaggeration would logically have undermined the point of his efforts. For this reason, we can gain quite a bit from his texts.

Later in the Middle Ages, galdr was banned. In the witch trials, right up to the seventeenth century in Denmark, it is still the word, promising evil or uttering of spells, that becomes the central part of the accusation in the trials. This is perhaps a remnant of the old faith.

In Anglo-Saxon England similar items such as swords with runic inscriptions have been found. One example is the Thames scramasax, which has text written in Anglo- Saxon runes. On one side it bears the name Beagnoth ᛒᛠᚷᚾᚩᚦ, which is thought to be the name of the owner. The find is from the tenth century.

In 1973, a section of human skull bone was discovered during an archaeological excavation in Ribe in Denmark. The skull is unusual in that it was inscribed with runes. This description has been interpreted by Niels Aage Nielsen in his edited edition of his 1983 book on runes, *Danske Runeindskrifter: et udvalg med kommentarer* (*Danish Runic Inscriptions: A Selection with Comments*) as: 'a worn amulet for protection against pain and enchanted swords'. It is understood that the 8 by 6 cm fragment of human skull was worn around the neck as a protective amulet. The runic inscription is not the only one to be found but is still one of very few from the Viking Age, although we have also found runic sticks with incantations for protection. It is interesting that many amulets are written in runes rather than in Latin, pointing to a strong belief in magical properties for these runic inscriptions.

How the runic inscription on the Ribe skull should be interpreted is much debated, six or seven translations of the inscription having been made. However, there is no doubt that it is an amulet that was supposed to ward off evil forces. The question then is whether it is a disease, or a weapon.

Another example of the use of runes and the belief in magical properties are the Spong Hill Urns (fifth Century) – three grave urns carrying the magical world 'alu'. 'Alu' is a common rune word used in the Iron Age. So, we can see that the Anglo-Saxons used runes in much the same way the Norsemen did. The word 'alu' is found on various items across England, and Scandinavia. In Denmark we also have an example of a person's name combined with the word 'alu' – Alugod was mentioned on a fibula or clothes pin, a find from the Danish Iron Age.

10

The Fylgja in the Norse World

Norse society had a concept of a Fylgja, mostly recognisable as a guardian spirit, which was an alter ego of every person and that took on the shape of an animal that had the same (or similar) personality as the person. A Danish folklore collector, Jens Kamp, had this explained to him.

> Every person has a spirit, a spirit, which always follows him, and which corresponds to the Old Norse Fylgja – whether it is evil or good, nothing is said about it.[39]

Jens Kamp, who relayed these stories, lived from 1845–1900 and the information was gathered in the nineteenth century for his publication *Danske Folkeminder*. The idea that a Fylgja, as an individual or family companion, still existed in the nineteenth century is fascinating, particularly given the Church's attempt to eradicate it during intervening centuries. Originating as a pre-Christian belief, during the medieval era a Fylgja, according to the Church, became a witch's familiar and the Völva, the seeresses of Norse mythology, became the wicked witches. In between the pre-Christian era and the modern age, the witch trials saw witches being burned at the stake. But in folklore and tradition, witches and Völvas, and Fylgjur and familiars were two different things and have been expressed in different ways, side by side. This is unsurprising as many of the old beliefs have survived in the shape of folklore, even though as the years have moved on the traditions existed in a more private form, away from the public sphere

In the pre-Christian world these Fylgjur were guardian spirits that protected an individual or family. In stories, they appear either as animal figures or as women – possibly female family goddesses. Fylgjur are usually invisible, but psychics can allegedly see a Fylgja when they are awake. Tradition has it that if a person sees a Fylgja, it could mean a harbinger of coming death.

It has been suggested by some that there is a connection between the Fylgja and Hamingja. Hamingja is another part of the self in Norse myth, who would aid a person and determine their luck. A large or powerful Hamingja was believed to be attached to royal and noble families. The Norse word 'hamingja' comes from the word 'hamr' and is a derivation of ganga – to walk – and relates to the idea of a change of person and the ability to transform. It is probably also connected with the amniotic membrane, and the belief that being born 'en caul' (when a baby is born whilst in the amniotic sac) is considered lucky and the child will have a protected life; it's comparable to being born in a 'victory shirt'.[57] In *Den store Danske* (The Great Danish Encyclopaedia), you can read:

> Hammer:
> The word relates to the notion of being able to change shape (Hamskifte), transform himself and appear in dreams or supernatural situations.[40]

It is often said that a Fylgja and Hamingja are a part of a person. Other associated terms in Nordic literature are: *Hamr* (shape or appearance; directly translated means form or skin); *Hugr*, (thoughts); *Fylgja* (follower); and *Hamingja* (happiness). Another similar term, *Hamram*, is explained in the dictionary for the Danish language:

> Ham-ram, adj. (Taken from old Norse, hamrammr; put together from old Norse 'Hamr', shape, and 'rammr', strong. That is, to have a strong hamr.)

The companion or the Fylgja was usually a noble or strong animal, such as the wolf, the bear or the deer. A Fylgja was understood to reflect the personality of the person, so strong personalities or warlike ones were particularly associated with wolves. A Fylgja also said something about social class, for instance the king could have a noble animal, such as the bear.

In graves around Scandinavia, sacrificed animals and animal skins have been found, as well as bear teeth. Kristina Jennbert has suggested that this animal may either reflect the personality of the person buried, or perhaps even represent a change to that person's spirit, where the dead person is transformed into the figure of his companion (Fylgja) on the journey to the Otherworld – the realm of the dead.

As time went on, the Fylgjur of the pre-Christian era would later become the witch's companion or familiar of the Middle Ages, as the Christian Church began to dismiss magical practices as demonic, asserting that a Fylgja was the devil, or a demon sent by the devil to help the witch with her deeds. As Christianity spread, the population certainly had the notion that the witch had a companion or familiar, or could transform, as it were, into an animal such as a hare. Across Europe, the hare was commonly considered an unclean animal and was often believed to be a witch's helper.

> In older times (at least still at the end of the last century) the common people in West Jutland did not eat hares, as well as baby veal. It is believed that the hare, which is also considered here in Denmark as one of the animals of the devil and trolls, – has been considered an unclean animal.[41]

But apparently, the notion of a Fylgja as a guiding rather than evil spirit did not totally disappear from belief systems, if Jens Kamp's collection of folk memories is to be believed.

Examples in early literature include Bjarkemál, an old Norse poem, where Bjarke sleeps in the hall, while his Fylgja or doppelgänger in animal shape is fighting outside. When Bjarke is finally woken up, the bear has disappeared.

> Hjalte gets a fire started in the house to burn down the hall. Then he discovers inside the hall Hrut's husband, Bjarke, lying in a deep sleep.
>
> Don't you bite, Bjarke!
>
> do Sleep Runes bind you?
>
> now go out with me
>
> before you burn!
>
> Bear with Fire is hunted,
>
> and now with fire Enemies:
>
> The cage flares high,
>
> The hall falls into gravel.[42]

This fits with the notion that the Fylgja comes out, or the shapeshifting happens in a trance or in a dreamlike state. Runes are also mentioned in connection with the transformation. Those skilled in sorcery could change shape, and runes could be used precisely for sorcery.

That the shapeshifting of men happened in a trance or sleep is also told in the story of Kveldulf.

We hear in *Egil's Saga* about the farmer, Kveldulf. He was a wise man, but towards evening he changed.

> Every day, on the other hand, when it was towards evening, he became so shy of people that they could not speak to him; early in the evening he went to bed. It was even believed that he was hamram (that means he could change his form or shape and take on a different nature than his own). Hence, he gained the name Kveldulf (evening wolf).[43]

The Fylgjur, therefore, were often seen as a companions or guardians but also could be the shape a person shapeshifted into to reach a certain state of mind. As we can see, trance was often considered a big part of this transformation. Even Odin was bound by these rules. When Odin desired to travel to other worlds, he lay like the dead, in a trance-like state, while his spirit travelled in the shape of an animal of some sort, such as birds, fish snakes etc. This trance-like state has many similarities to the shamanic state, or *hamr*, and is characterised by a temporary, deep slumber where spirit leaves the body, with the purpose of gaining knowledge and information.

11

The Gods of the Germanic Tribes

We mostly learn about the Germanic gods from the Icelandic Sagas from the thirteenth and fourteenth centuries. Of course, the texts are written from a Christian perspective, so we must therefore analyse them from this standpoint. However, archaeology and other texts describing the Viking faith points to it being informative of pre-Christian beliefs and practices.

The principal gods of both the Germanic people and the Norse/Vikings were firstly the Aesir/Æsir and secondly the Vanir. The Anglo-Saxons would have worshipped the same principal group of gods as the later Vikings, as did the rest of the Germanic tribes. The Aesir/Æsir resided in a place called Asgard on the top of the world tree, Yggdrasil. These two groups of gods were mutually at war at one stage, exchanging hostages, and eventually concluding a peace treaty. With the hostages given by the Vanir was the god Njord, the god of the sea, and his two children Frey and Freya.

Odin

Odin was the leader of the principal gods, the Aesir, but he went under several names, for instance All Father or the High One. He was the god of knowledge, war, battle, victory, sorcery, poetry, and frenzy. His name means 'Lord of Frenzy' or ecstasy. Odin was especially the god of kings and the upper class. Several kings of the Norse area, such as the Danish royal Scylding dynasty, claimed to be descended from Odin, the Scyldings being mentioned in the poem Beowulf. The very same is said of Hengest and Horsa, reportedly the very first Anglo-Saxons arriving on the shores of Britain:

> The two first commanders are said to have been Hengest and Horsa... They were the sons of Victgilsus, whose father was

> Vacta, son of Woden, from whose stock the royal race of many provinces deduces their original.[44]

The oldest mention of Odin is found with the Vinderlev treasure discovered in 2020 (from Jutland, in Denmark). It consists of gold bracteates or little gold discs, thought to be magical gold pendants with mythological motifs, and has been dated to the fifth century AD. According to the Danish runologist, Lisbeth Imer, who has examined the treasure, it is the first solid evidence we have of Odin being worshipped in the fifth century, being 150 years earlier than a brooch found in southern Germany, which dates to the second half of the sixth century AD. Both finds prove an earlier belief in Odin than previously reckoned and closes some of the gaps between the time of Tacitus and that of the later migration period when the Anglo-Saxons settled in Britain. The Danish tribe is already mentioned as early as the sixth century by Jordanes who operated as far away as Rivanna, in Italy. His interest was in telling people about the origins of the Gothic people in Scandinavia, from whom he was descended. At the same time, he describes some of the other tribes, such as the Danes. The finds also show a widespread geographical belief in Odin, as the two finds are very far apart. This would suggest that the Anglo-Saxons and Jutes arriving in Britain from today's Denmark and northern parts of Germany and Frisia also worshipped Odin as one of their gods. We can also see this thread in certain place names in areas of England such as Wambrook, Somerset ('Woden's Brook'), Wansdyke (Woden's Dyke/Ditch) in Wiltshire or Woden Hill in Hampshire or Wampool in Hampshire (Woden's Pool), to name a few examples. Wednesday, in English, also means Woden's day.

Pendants have also been found in recent years which are believed to represent the god Woden/Odin with his twin ravens, Hugin and Munin, and can be compared to the helmet plate from Sutton Hoo, which depicts ravens, almost certainly referencing Odin. Similar pendants have been found in Denmark depicting a male face with two hornlike features on the helmets that end in birds, again thought to depict Odin with his ravens.

As discussed earlier, both Odin and Freya were masters of seidr. Odin, in his function as a shaman, was capable of shapeshifting – he would lie dead while he travelled as a bird, fish or other being into all nine worlds of Yggdrasil.

According to Norse prophecy, at Ragnarök (the Norse apocalypse; the Old Norse word 'Ragnarök' means 'Fate of the Gods'), Odin is supposed to be swallowed by the Fenrir wolf, the son of Loki, the trickster. It was also believed that Odin, along with his brothers, created and gave life to the first two humans, Ask and Embla. Ask was created from an ash tree and Embla from an elm tree.

Thor

Thor was the son of Odin, a thunder god and a god of fertility, making him especially attractive to the common people farming the land. Amulets in the shape of a hammer, especially used in the late Viking Age, have been found in all of Scandinavia and in the areas where they settled. Thor's hammer and similar amulets were considered protective charms and bringers of good luck.

According to the myth, Thor had a hammer made by dwarf brothers Sindri and Brokkr. Loki had cut off Thor's wife's hair (her name was Sif), so Thor seized Loki and threatened to break every bone in his body if he did not get the hair back on her head. Loki went to the dark elves (the dwarfs) and had them make Sif new hair. Loki then bet his head with Brokkr and Sindri that Sindri could not make three equal items 'Equal in virtue to these'. The dwarfs were known for being highly skilled in blacksmithing and having great knowledge, creating several of the objects of the Norse gods, including the three that resulted from this challenge: Gullinbursti (Freyr's boar), Draupnir (Odin's ring) and finally Thor's hammer, Mjølnir. To deceive the two dwarfs, Loki turned himself into a fly and stung the dwarf Brokkr, in an attempt to disturb them in the smithing process, so they could not finish their work, but he did not succeed.

> Straightway the fly settled between Brokkr's eyes and stung his eyelid, but when the blood fell into his eyes so he could not see, then he clutched at it with his hand as swiftly as he could, – while the bellows grew flat, – and he swept the fly from him. Then the smith came thither and said that it had come near to spoiling all that was in the hearth. Then he took from the forge a hammer.[45]

Also, according to the myth, the dwarfs are created from Birmir's blood and the limbs of Blain. These are different names for the giant Ymir from which the world was created. The names of the dwarfs are mentioned in the *Poetic Edda*, and the creation of the dwarfs is mentioned in *The Völuspa*. They lived underground in mountains and stones or mounds in the landscape. The dwarfs seem to be synonymous with the Svartálfar and the Dökkálfar, dark álfar, or dark elves. We are told they live in Nidavellir. They are said not to be able to handle sunlight. Their world is also called Myrkheimr – 'Myrk' means dark and 'heimr' means home, thus meaning 'The world of darkness'.

Thor's wife, Sif, was a Jötunn or giantess and goddess of fertility, grain, family, and marriage. Even though Odin has giants in his ancestry, he is not classified as a giant but as a primal god. His lineage starts with his grandfather

Buri – the first god was released from the ice by the licking of the cow Audhumla. His father, Borr, married the giantess Bestl, mixing the forces of chaos with the ordered world. The ordered world is also linked to the world of chaos, when Odin mixes his blood with Loki, thus making them blood brothers. This is how Loki, a giant (or Jötunn) came to live among the gods, the creators of the ordered world. Thor's greatest foe was Jörmungandr, the Midgard Worm/ Serpent and child of Loki and the giantess Angrboda. The serpent, having been thrown by the gods into the ocean, lies in the water biting its own tale, entirely surrounding the world. The Midgard Worm is the arch enemy of Thor, and a Völva has prophesied that they are to meet at Ragnarök, where they will battle once more and where both are to perish.

Frigg

Odin's wife was Frigg. As well as being the goddess of motherhood and the mother of Balder, she was also central in the stories. In the sagas she is described as the equal of Odin when it comes to seeing events in the world.

In several myths, Frigg and Freya are in many ways described as almost alike. This has led to speculation that they may originally have been the same goddess, but the question of joint or separate identities cannot currently be resolved because the sagas reveal them as two different goddesses with differing properties.

Frigg owns the horse Hovvarpnir, which, in Norse mythology, is one of the horses that can fly. She gave it to Gna, who is Frigg's messenger. Balder is described as the most beautiful among the gods and is known as the god of justice.

In *Grímnismál*, Frigg challenges Odin. *Grímnismál* is the fourth divine poem in the *Codex Regius*. The poem is one of the primary sources for Norse mythology and is considered part of the *Elder Edda*. The poem is also preserved in the *Codex Regius*.

The poem is narrated by Grímnir, one of Odin's many disguises. The very name Grímnir also indicates a mask or hood. King Geirrød tortures Grímnir, which becomes a fatal mistake for him, as Odin makes him fall on his own sword. The poem is mainly written in verse.

Loki

Loki/Loke is the trickster in Norse mythology. He is the son of Fárbauti, a Jötunn, and of Laufey, an Ásynja (a female goddess), as well as being a blood brother of Odin, because he has mixed blood with him. Loki's several children include Narfi or Nari. He is also the father of Hel, Fenrir, and Jörmungandr (the Midgard Worm/Serpent). The mother of Hel, Fenrir and Jörmungandr is the giantess Angrboda. Yet again we have a clear connection between the Jötnar with the chaos forces of nature which cannot be controlled. These three children of Loki play a part in the coming Ragnarök. Odin throws Hel into Niflheim, which is a place for people dying of sickness and old age and gives her nine worlds there. The realm of Hel is the place you go after death if you are not selected to go to Valhalla or Folksvangr, both honourable afterlife destinations.

Loki's son, Fenrir, was a monstrous wolf in Norse mythology, and many have heard of the myth surrounding the Fenrir wolf in which the gods attempt several times to chain him, but they fail until Tyr places his hand in Fenrir's mouth, losing one hand in the process.

Here again the dwarfs play a role as they are asked to make the chain Gleipnir, with which to chain Fenrir, using fish breath, birds' spittle, bears' sinews, mountains' roots, cats' paw noises and women's beards. The gods place a sword across Fenrir's mouth to prevent him from biting and bind him in a cave in Jötunheim, one of the nine worlds of Yggdrasil. Jötunheim is, as the name reveals, the world of the Jötnar or the giants.

The Völuspa and *The Younger Edda* by Snorri Sturluson both mention the myth of Ragnarök. This is the final battle, according to Norse myth, between the gods and Jötnar/giants, in which most of those fighting can and will be killed before the world is reborn and starts anew. Ragnarök begins with natural disasters, one of which, the Finbul winter, comprises three years of deep winter. We can say it constitutes the final battle between the forces of chaos and the ordered world.

The Finbul winter is believed to have been an actual event worked into the myth. In the year AD 536 a volcanic eruption darkened the skies of the northern hemisphere. Later, in AD 540, another eruption caused further starvation and population decline. Excavations in archaeology show the abandonment of farms as a consequence of these volcanic disasters.[46]

Loki, as we have seen, is something of a trickster – a wild card if you will, not evil per se. In *The Younger Edda* he is described as beautiful to look at and wicked. He might have got that description as a comparison to the Judaic/Christian Lucifer, since the author was Christian and, as mentioned, writing in a Christian context.

> Loke is nimble and beautiful to look at but has a malicious and very changeable nature.[47]

Depictions of Loki have been found on stones from the Viking Age near towns in Denmark (Snaptun) and England (Gainford and Kirkby Stephen). According to sources, the Kirkby stone is supposed to be the only depiction of Loki in Britain. It has been examined by Danish experts:

> This is an Anglo-Danish cross-shaft of the tenth century [recently dated by experts from Denmark] made of pink sandstone that depicts Loki. Loki is a figure in Norse mythology with a status like the gods. It is often said to be the only carving of Loki to have been found in Britain although some believe that Loki is also depicted on the Gosforth cross and on a carving found at Gainford in Durham. The ninth and tenth centuries were the 'Viking age' when many Danes and Norwegians settled in Cumbria alongside the existing Celtic and Northumbrian (English) populations. During this time, they abandoned their 'old religion' and became Christians. Kirkby Stephen is a placename of Danish origin. It is believed that the first church to build in Kirkby Stephen was constructed in about 850 – probably preceding the settlement of the area by the Danes and Norwegians. The 'Loki Stone' may therefore be a Christian cross-over piece depicting Loki as the devil with horns.[48]

This cross-over between the two belief systems is not uncommon. Beliefs did not change overnight, and a mixture of two ideas or faiths is often seen on such things as artwork, and gravestones. Thus, perhaps as we can see with the writings in the saga, Loki seems to have been made somehow to look like Lucifer. Additionally, the Danes did not worship the suffering Christ until many years had passed, although the Norsemen did convert to Christianity over time. But the Christ they worshipped had many similarities to Odin, being the strong, warlike victorious Christ. For this reason, doubt has been cast on the Christ-like figure on the Jellinge rune stone in Denmark, where Harald Bluetooth declares that he has made all Danes Christians. It has been suggested that perhaps it really is Odin we are looking at, although the stance of the figure looks similar to Christ on the cross.

For his part, Loki constantly breaks conventional, natural and social norms. In one such case he changes gender and turns himself into a mare. In this state he gives birth to Odin's horse, Sleipnir. In many ways he is the symbol of the chaos forces or forces of nature beyond human control. Like Odin and many of the gods, he is a shapeshifter. Often creating trouble, he is, for example, to blame for the death of Balder.

However, in most cases when Loki creates trouble, hard-pressed by the gods he is able to regain a peaceful balance – although usually trying to save his own skin, he is described as a bit of a coward! In the tale of the kidnapping of Idunn, Loki's behaviour lands him in the hands of the giant Thiazi.

Idunn is the goddess of youth, who guards the apples that keep the gods young. The story of her kidnapping is told in *Skáldskaparmál,* part of the *Prose Edda* or *The Younger Edda*, believed to have been written by Snorri Sturluson. Here, Loki is blamed for trying to save his own skin. The story begins when three of the Aesir, Odin, Loki and Hœnir, were on a trip together in an area where the food was very scarce. They finally find an ox to eat but the cooking does not go as planned. The giant, Thiazi, in disguise as an eagle, had put a spell on the ox they tried to cook.

> Then the eagle said: 'If ye are willing to give me my fill of the ox, then it will cook in the fire'. They assented to this. Then he let himself float down from the tree and a lighted by the fire, and forthwith at the very first took unto himself the two hams of the ox, and both shoulders. Then Loki was angered, snatched up a great pole, brandished it with all his strength, and drove it at the eagle's body. The eagle plunged violently at the blow and flew up, so that the pole was fast to the eagle's back, and Loki's hands to the other end of the pole. The eagle flew at such a height that Loki's feet down below knocked against stones and rock-heaps and trees, and he thought his arms would be torn from his shoulders. He cried aloud, entreating the eagle urgently for peace; but the eagle declared that Loki should never be loosed, unless he would give him his oath to induce Idunn to come out of Ásgard with her apples.[49]

Loki agrees to the terms but omits mentioning this to his travelling companions. Loki later lures Idunn outside of Asgard with the promise of showing her some apples equal to hers. Here Thiazi, in his eagle plumage, carries her away. Soon enough the gods notice Idunn's absence as they begin to age. They start to inquire and find out that she had last been seen with Loki.

> Thereupon Loki was seized and brought to the Thing, and was threatened with death, or tortures; when he had become well frightened, he declared that he would seek after Idunn in Jötunheim.[50]

As we are told in this very story, Loki is both the cause of the trouble and the one who restores order, but all due to his selfishness in saving his own hide. In the end Idunn returns to the Aesir.

In the course of this tale, Loki transformed into a falcon, turning Idunn into a nut in order to carry her away. As nuts have been found in graves of Anglo-Saxons and in the west and south Germanic area, religious historian, Hilda Ellis Davidson, has suggested that this might have been tied to a fertility cult. It is difficult to say if this is the case, but there is a lot to merit it, including that nuts are the fruit of trees and are also seen to be part of the myths in the Celtic area.

As for apples, some scholars believe that their possible role as a symbol of fertility is borrowed from contact with the Romans. However, Gro Steinland, Professor of Religion at Oslo University, points out that wild apples have been found in the Oseberg grave and the many mentions of apples in mythology must mean they were an old, incorporated symbol in Norse mythology. Both could be right. Perhaps it is a mixture.

Loki is also the father of Hel, the goddess of death, ruler of Helheim, the Norse world of death. Yet again we might in this myth find some connection or mixture of Christian and pre-Christian beliefs in this tale of Hel. Though there is no fire and brimstone in the Norse Hel, it is a place of gloom and suffering. Everything around Hel has names associated with disaster – Hungr is the name of her dish, famine is the name of her knife, and her bed is named Kör, meaning sickbed. Hel is the place where people dying of sickness and old age go in the Viking Age.

Bragi

Bragi is the Norse god of poetry, commonly known as the Skaldic god, and was synonymous with wisdom and inspiration. In *Gylfaginning*, part of *The Younger Edda*, we are told this about him:

> One is called Bragi: he is renowned for wisdom, and most of all for fluency of speech and skill with words. He knows most of skaldship, and after him skaldship is called bragr, and from his name that one is called bragr-man or -woman, who possesses eloquence surpassing others, of women or of men. His wife is Idunn.[51]

In one place in *Skáldskaparmál*, Bragi is named as a son of Odin.

The Skald/Skjald were professional history tellers in the Viking Age and medieval periods, known for their Skaldic poetry – a highly ornate form of Old Norse court poetry. An important part of the king's household, their task was to recount the past, including the king's heroic deeds.

Frey and Freya

According to various medieval sources, the Vanir and the Aesir were at war at some point. When a peace agreement was reached, they exchanged hostages. Among them were Frey and Freya who were sent to the Aesir along with their father Njord, the sea god. Both Frey and Freya are significant in the stories.

Frey/Freyr (meaning lord in Norse) is usually associated with prosperity, kingship, peace, fertility, and good harvests. He is the brother of Freya and son of Njord and is from Vanaheim. Vanaheim is the home of the Vanir gods. Frey was also Lord of Álfheim, the realm of the elves. According to Adam of Bremen, Frey was particularly revered in Sweden at Uppsala. The Swedish royal house saw itself as descendant from Frey.

As part of the peace treaty, the Aesir sent Hönir and Mimir as to the Vanir as hostages. Hönir is said to have given man reason and Mimir was known for his wisdom and knowledge. It is unclear whether Hönir is Vili, the brother of Odin. In *The Völuspa* and the *Poetic Edda*, Hönir helps Odin, but in *Gylfaginning*, Vili and Vé are mentioned instead. Thus, it is possible that Hönir is another name for Vili.

> Soul they had not, sense they had not,
> Heat nor motion, nor goodly hue;
> Soul gave Odin, sense gave Hönir,
> Heat gave Lothar and goodly hue.[52]

According to the story, Hönir was made chief upon their arrival in Vanaheim. But he was indecisive and relied on the council of Mimir. Soon the Vanir started to believe that they had been cheated by the Aesir with the hostage exchange. They grabbed Mimir, cut off his head and sent it back to the Aesir. By embalming the head and with magical formulas, Odin made sure that the head remained alive, so he had access to the wisdom of Mimir. In *The Völuspa* Odin sacrifices his one eye so he can gain knowledge by drinking from the well of Mimir.

Alone I sat when the old one sought me,
The terror of the gods and gazes in mine eyes;
'What hast thou to ask, Why comest thou hither?
Odin, I know where thine eye is hidden.'
I know where Odin's eye is hidden,
Deep in the wide-famed well of Mimir;
Mead from the pledge of Othin each mom
Does Mimir drink, would you know yet more?[53]

Freya, the twin sister of Frey, was the one who taught Odin galdr and seidr. Freya is also the archetype of the Völva, the Norse seeress or witch who could predict the future. Galdr, a spell or incantation in old Norse, was performed before any battle was joined. Usually performed in connection with rites, it is a form of sorcery, a spell said out loud. In the medieval period in Denmark, this type of incantation was prohibited as the Church tried to root out Pagan practice of various kinds.

Freya also receives half of those who have fallen in battle. That half of the fallen go to Folksvangr, Freya's realm, as depicted in *Gylfaginning*:

Fólkvangr't is called, | where Freyja rules
Degrees of seats in the hall;
Half the kill | she keepeth each day,
And half Odin hath

And in *Grímnismál*

The ninth is Folkvang, | where Freyja decrees,
Who shall have seats in the hall;
The half of the dead | each day does she choose,
And half does Odin have.[54]

Freya supposedly has the first pick of half the fallen warriors before Odin takes his half to Valhöll or Valhalla.

As mentioned, there is often comparison between Freya and the goddess Frigg, the wife of Odin, in some of the Norse myths. Although there may have been some crossover at some point, in the sagas they are clearly two entities with different roles.

12

Other Female Goddesses/ Spirits of the Norse Myths

The Völvas, the powerful seeresses in Norse and Viking society, were in good company with the many powerful and female deities that can be found in Norse myth. Three of the most prominent female spirits are discussed here.

The Norns

The Norns (Old Norse: norn; plural: nornir) were a group of goddesses in Norse mythology who were associated with fate. The best-known Norns in mythology are Urðr (Urd), Verðandi (Verdande), and Skuld, whose names are traditionally translated as past, present, and future. The name Urðr is related to the Anglo-Saxon wyrd, or weird, a concept equivalent to the Norse concept of fate. Wyrd is an old English word meaning fate or destiny, weird being a more modern version of the word.

The sources indicate that, in addition to these three, countless Norns were imagined who determined the fate of all types of beings. For example, when a child was born, a Norn was present to determine its fate in life. The Norns' function could thus be seen as both beneficent and harmful, as some people were given a good and long life, while others a short and difficult life.

The Norns are mentioned in both *The Völuspa* and *The Younger Edda.*

The Valkyries

The name itself is a clear indicator of what these beings are – the name means chooser of the slain. The Valkyrjur (singular: valkyrja), commonly anglicised as Valkyries, are fearsome female spirits who serve and assist Odin by selecting the dead warriors on the battlefield to be carried to Valhöll/Valhalla. In the Viking Age these beings were rather gloomy creatures who used magic to ensure their preferred warrior dies in battle. Darraðarljóð is a skaldic poem in Old Norse found in Chapter 157 of *Njáls Saga*, recounting the vision of a man named Dörruð, in which twelve Valkyries weave and choose who is to be slain at the Battle of Clontarf. The poem inform us that twelve Valkyries are weaving the fate of man before the battle with human entrails.

'Dorrud's Song'
Blood rains
from the cloudy web
on the broad loom
of slaughter.
The web of man
grey as armor
is now being woven;
the Valkyries
will cross it
with a crimson weft.

The warp is made
Of human entrails;
Human heads
Are used as heddle-weights;
Hed heddle rods are blood-wet spears;
The shafts are iron-bound
and arrows are the shuttles.
With swords we will weave this web of battle.[55]

In Scandinavia, various figures have been found believed to be depicting the Valkyries. Valkyrie jewelry which has been unearthed comes in different variants – either as free-standing single figures (like the Valkyrie from Kirke Hyllinge) or as a combination of rider + horse + upright figure. One such, with rider and horse, were found at Lake Tissø, the sacrificial lake in Denmark. The Valkyries are closely connected to other goddesses of Norse myth such as the Disir, the Norns and the Völva. Freya, sometimes called Vanadís (meaning goddess of the Vanir), was closely tied to the Valkyrie, as the goddess of fertility, war and death.

In Anglo-Saxon sources, the related words Wælcyrge and Wælcyrie appear. This suggests a common early Germanic tradition. Dominicis Diebus, the Proclamation of 1020, recalls a list of God-hated sinners, and showcases the Valkyrie among them:

> For ðam þe ealle biscopas secgað, þæt hit swyþe deop wið God to betanne, þæt man aðas oððe wedd tobrece. eac hy us furðor lærað, þæt we sceolon eallan magene & eallon myhton þone ecan mildan God inlice secan, lufian & weorðian & ælc unriht ascunian, ðæt synd mægslagan & morðslagan & mansworan & wiccean & wælcyrian & æwbrecan & syblegeru.
>
> For it is as the bishops say, that it is very much with God to be amended if one breaks an oath or a pledge. Further, they declare that we ought, with all our might and all our main, seek and love and honor God, who is mild, and all of us must avoid unrighteousness, the deeds of kin-slayers, manslayers and murderers and perjurers and witches and Valkyries and adulterers and incests. In aligning his own politics and religion with that polity and faith already present in Anglo-Saxon England, Cnut likewise maligns the wiccean & wælcyrian as enemies of the faith, the state, and the social fabric of the nation as a whole.[56]

In this we are informed that these beings, the Wælcyrian, are considered an enemy of the faith. They are mentioned alongside witches. The cunning woman or the Völva eventually became the wicked witches of the medieval era and the Valkyries of the Norse myths were often connected with the Völva. Whether the word Wælcyrian is borrowed from the Norse or is an Anglo-Saxon word pointing to a wider Germanic tradition is debated.

Dísir

The Dísir are a group of supernatural, female beings in Norse mythology, often appearing as guardian spirits, fate goddesses, or ancestral spirits. Dísir, the plural form of Old Norse, Dís, means 'lady' or 'female guardian'. They can be both good and evil, are closely associated with fertility and the Valkyries, and were honored at dísablót festivals, the exact timing of which varied by region.

The Disir are mentioned numerous times in the sagas. One such mention is in the *Grímnismál*. Here King Geirrød's death is by Grímnís (Odin in disguise); his death is by Odin's hand but fulfills the wrath of the Dísir who had plotted his death.

> The fallen by the sword
> Ygg shall now have;
> Thy life is now run out
> Wroth with the are the dísir:
> Odin thou now shall see:
> Draw near to me if thou can.

The Dísir also seem to have a connection to the ancestors and were often regarded as female spirits watching over their descendants; they are also sometimes associated with the Fylgja.

The Anglo-Saxon counterpart to the Dísir blót is the Modranith, 'Mothers night', that took place around the same time as the winter solstice and has a clear link to the continental matron cult which resemble the varied spirits that the Dísir represent. Bede mentions the Modranith in his eighth-century work. The matrons were female spirits, and, as with the Dísir, are connected with ancestry. Another Anglo-Saxon word that has links to the continental Saxons is the word 'Ides' (Old Saxon Idis). This word refers to a noble woman or a supernatural being similar to that of the Dísir.

13

Skalds, Scops and the Tul or Thul (Poet/Wise Man)

The Skalds (Skjalds in Danish) were highly respected poets and storytellers of the Viking Age, often residing in the courts of kings and chieftains. Before stories were written down, the Skalds passed down traditions orally, most famously in the form of poetry.

Associated with the 'Skaldship' is the Norse word Tul, Thul or Pulr, meaning poet and wise man. Tul is a title which seems to have contained a priest-like function. The function of the Tul is connected to ritualistic reciting, speaking or singing of words, thereby having a connection to the worship of the gods. The Tul is also connected to Odin and thereby poetry.

In *The Hávámál*, the chair of the Tul is at the well of Urdr, a well likely named after one of the Norns. The Norns weaved the destinies of men and gods alike, thus connecting the Tul/Thul and the knowledge of the Skald to that of fate. Religious practice and customs were based on oral traditions and the Tul and Skald therefore played an important role in society.

However, Tul and Skald are not entirely the same, although it may be that the Skald eventually became the substitute for the Tul. In the medieval period the religious function would have been lost as the Norse countries became Christian.

Since the verses were composed using strict metrical rules, it is believed that many of the poems have survived more or less in their original form from the Viking Age where they were orally told. Most of the verses surviving are from the Icelandic sagas and are about the Norwegian kings. This is because Iceland was closely linked to Norway. We know that the Skalds were composing at the Danish and Swedish courts as well, but unlike the Norwegian and Icelandic poems, these compositions have not survived.

The Tale of the Skaldik Mead

Norse 'Skjaldemjød' (Skaldik Mead), is a mead which makes you a poet or wise man.

> After the peace treaty was concluded the gods would not let the peace mark go to waste.
>
> When they parted, the gods did not want to let that sign of peace pass away but created a man from it by the name Kvasir, who was so wise that no one could ask him anything that he could not answer. He then travelled around the world to teach people wisdom. Once he came to visit with two Dwarves, the brothers Fjalar and Galar. They lured him aside, killed him, and let his blood run in three vessels. The kettle was called Odrerir, while the vessels were called Son and Bodn. They mixed the blood with honey, and from this, a mead arose, which has the property that anyone who drinks from it becomes a Skjald or a wise man. To the Æsir they said that Kvasir had been suffocated by his great wisdom.[57]

The dwarves lost the skaldic mead to the giant Suttungr, who was the son of the giant Gilling, who drowned after a sailing trip with the dwarves, after which they had killed his wife. When Suttungr threatened to kill the dwarves, they offered the mead to him if he spared their lives. Suttungr agreed and kept the mead in three containers. He had his daughter Gunnlod keep watch over the precious cargo.

Odin often travelled in disguise and on this trip, he sought out Baugi, Suttungr's brother. Having heard of the mead, Odin wanted it for himself and agreed with Baugi to work for him for a year for a promise of a drink of Suttungr's mead. After the year passed, they went to Suttungr who refused to let him have the drink.

> Odin called himself Bölverkr in Baug's presence; He offered to undertake nine men's work for Baugi and demanded for his wages one drink of Suttungr's mead.[58]

Odin sleeps three nights with Suttungr's daughter, Gunnlod, and drinks three drinks from the containers.

> Bölverkr proceeded to the place where Gunnlod was and lay with her three nights, and then she gave him leave to drink three draughts of the mead. In the first draught, he drank every drop out of Odrerir; and in the second, he emptied Bodn; and in the third, Són; and then he had all the mead.[59]

Odin then transformed himself into an eagle and escaped in that shape. But he was close to being caught by Suttungr, which is when he spat up all the mead, some going backwards. This is said to be the mead that caused poor Skalds. He gave the good mead to the Aesir and those men worthy of composing. The story of the mead going backwards seems like an attempt to explain poorly talented Skalds.

> But Odin gave the mead of Suttungr to the Æsir and to those men who possess the ability to compose. Therefore, we call poesy Odin's booty and find, and his drink and gift, and the Drink of the Aesir.[60]

That Odin initially had all the mead, meant he gained all the knowledge and wisdom contained in it. Giving it to Aesir and men alike meant giving knowledge and wisdom to those who compose and are Skalds. We hear the same story in *The Hávámál*:

> I visited the old giant, now I have come back,
> I did not get much there from being silent;
> With many words, I spoke to my advantage
> In Suttungr's hall.
> Gunnlod gave me from the golden throne
> A drink of the precious mead;
> A poor reward I let her have in return,
> For her open-heartedness,
> For her heavy spirit.[61]

In *The Hávámál* we are also informed that Odin gains knowledge of sorcery or spells from the mead:

> Nine mighty spells I learnt from the famous son
> of Bolthor, Bestla's father,
> and I got a drink from the precious mead
> poured from Odrerir.[62]

Odrerir refers to the kettle containing the mead as seen earlier from *The Younger Edda.*

Heiðrún or Heidrun is the goat that produces mead which the Einherjars are served. Heidrun feeds from the tree Læraðr (Laerad), which stands on the top of Valhöll/Valhalla and is mentioned several times in the sagas, such as in *Grímnismál*, *Gylfaginning* and *Hyndluljóð.*

In the sagas as well as *The Gesta Danorum: History of the Danes*, we are also told that the royals and nobles are taught to play instruments. In this particular story from *Gesta Danorum* about Hød and Balder, Hød playing the instrument could affect the emotions of men. The story also tells us how important it was to be able to play an instrument.

> Regarding the abilities and inclinations of the soul, he was far ahead of his young years. In playing the lute and the lyre, he was superior, and he was also adept at the lyre and all kinds of stringed instruments, so that with his tones he could turn people's feelings as he pleased, and knew how to arouse joy or sorrow, pity or Resentment in their souls, so he soon tickled their ears, soon filled them with terror.[63]

We can understand from this that being taught an instrument was an essential part of the upbringing of the royals and nobles. The most common type of stringed instrument to have survived from this period is the lyre. These have been found in England at royal burials such as Taplow and Sutton Hoo, as well as in lesser graves. The Ribe lyre is Denmark's oldest stringed instrument, found in 2018 during excavations in Ribe's oldest Viking settlement (around AD 720). The well-preserved part of the instrument comes from a marketplace and is evidence of advanced culture and musical life in the Viking Age.

Yet again we find similarities between the Anglo-Saxon and Norse culture prior to the Viking Age. Sutton Hoo is from the early seventh century, hence falling close to the same timeline as the Ribe lyre.

The Scops

The Scops are similar to the bards or the skalds, and appear in the courts of the mediaeval Saxon rulers.

> Music was seen by our early Anglo-Saxon forefather settlers as something from another world or realm and could be 'magic' in itself or imbued with magical properties.[64]

In the Anglo-Saxon period the Scops were the primary source of entertainment and told stories of the deeds of warriors and kings. They were not necessarily required to speak of real-life events, nor to keep their tales true to fact. They narrated stories about happenings in the world and would have known stories not just from their own kingdom but also from other areas as well. The mention of magic in connection with the scops gives them a similar standing to that of the Tul.

A skilled Scop could become a court poet, as mentioned in Beowulf.

> now and then the poet raised his voice, resonant in Heorot... Then Hrothgar, leader in battle, was entertained with music – harp and voice in harmony. The strings were plucked, many a song rehearsed, when it was the turn of Hrothgar's poet to please men at the mead bench, perform in the hall... Thus was the lay sung, the song of the poet. The hall echoed with joy; waves of noise broke out along the benches...

14

Festivals in the Norse World

It was believed there were at least four fixed blót (feasts) sacrifices around the year: winter solstice, spring equinox, summer solstice and autumn equinox. Besides these four, other blót sacrifices also took place in times of crisis, such as famine or war. A blót is a ritual which usually included sacrifices of various kinds. As discussed previously, these sacrifices could be either animals or humans. Of course we cannot say how exaggerated the accounts are, but there are archaeological finds which can confirm the sacrifice of both animals and humans.

In the Viking age, one of the most important celebrations was Midwinter. The period from October to April was considered winter, thus the Midwinter celebration was in the middle of January. At this point, the wheel of the year turned towards lighter times – a rebirth of a new year. The celebrations began at the winter solstice. We are brought up with the notion that Yule or Jól is a Christian celebration but in fact the Vikings celebrated Yule. In Scandinavia, the word for Christmas is still Jul which derives from Jól, a plural word which means a row of festivals, so the celebrations were a row of feasts probably starting around the winter solstice.

The Arab chronicler, Ibrahim ibn Ahmed at-Tartuschi, tells how the winter solstice was celebrated in the town of Haithabu, an important trading town of the Vikings, founded by a Danish king named Godfredus in Latin, Gudrød in Danish. This was done by sacrificing animals to the gods.

> They celebrate a feast where they all come together to honor the gods and to eat and drink. He who slaughters a sacrificial animal sets up stakes at the door of his courtyard and places the sacrificial animal on it, whether it is a bullock or a ram or a he-goat or a pig, so that the people may know that he sacrifices to the honor of his god.[65]

In *Håkon the Good's Saga* the king visited some farmers who demanded he was to do a blót, meaning he was to sacrifice to the gods for 'til àrs ok fridar' (for a good year and peace).

> But he who made the feast and was the chieftain, was to bless the cup and all the blót food; he had first to bless Odin's cup, that were to drink for the king's victory and power – and then for Njord's cup and Frey's cup for prosperity and peace. It was very common to drink Brage's cup next; you also drank the cups to honor your dead relatives, and it was called 'memorial'.[66]

Here we also see the importance of Brage, the Norse god of skaldic art, as they are to drink from his cup as well.

In the same saga we are told that the people expected the king and his chieftains to maintain the blót. King Håkon is threatened with a riot if he does not celebrate the blót as it has been done in the past.

> When it was asked, earl Sigurd answered and said that 'it is King Haakon's will to agree with you peasants, and never to part with your friendship'. The peasants say that they want the king to do the blót for year and peace, as his father did. Then the unrest stops, and the thing ends.[67]

In *The Saga of Hervör and Heidrek*, we are told of the sacrifice of a boar at Yule.

> King Heidrek worshipped Frey and promised to offer him the biggest boar he could get; this was considered to be so sacred that over its brushes all important matters were to be judged. The boar was to be sacrificed as a sacrificial offering, and on Yule (Christmas) Eve it was to be brought to the hall before the king; then people used to put their hands on its brushes and make holy vows.[68]

As mentioned, Frey was a god of fertility for the Germanic people and the boar or the pig was a symbol of fertility. It is therefore not surprising that the pig plays a central place in the sacrifices at Yule. In the sources we are also told it is the women who took care of the sacrifices. This would be a so-called Gyðja, a female cult leader. In Norse, the masculine form is goði. The goði, or gothi was a religious leader and chieftain in the Norse area. A gothi is mentioned on the

Glavendrup Runestone, the Flemløse Runestone and the Helnæs Runestone, all on the island of Funen, in Denmark – their function, as a Pagan priest, would have been a common one among the Germanic tribes across Europe. In Iceland in the pre-Christian era, they had more power than most places. The word is believed to derive from the word goð, which means 'god'. The Anglo-Saxons arriving in England would have had similar beliefs though their importance and power varied from place to place.

Bede mentions a Coifi in his *Ecclesiastical History of the English People*. According to him, the Coifi was the high priest of Wotan to King Edwin of Northumbria. The Coifi would likely have had the same function as the goði.

Vetrnætr, which literally translates to 'winter nights', was a Norse winter festival honouring the ancestors and therefore it has a lot of similarities with that of Samhain. It was a time marking the end of summer and the start of winter, and similar to Samhain, it was believed that at this time of year the veil between the worlds was thinner and fires were lit to ward off evil spirits. Similar beliefs are later found in the Christian era on Valpurgis night, or the night before 1 May, and midsummer eve. On Valpurgis night in Denmark, it was tradition to make a bonfire with what was called wild fire – two pieces of wood rubbed against each other. They believed that the bonfire would scare of evil spirits, witches and Otherworldly beings that were particularly active and close by.

The Sigr blót was held at the fourth full moon in April and celebrated the coming of summer. Sigr or Victory blót was a sacrifice to Odin and Frey and was aimed at securing successful raids, travel, trade and a good harvest. At this time of the year the season for Viking raids started and therefore Odin would also have been called upon as the god of war.

Sumarmál marks the first day of summer and traditionally was considered a day of celebration. The festivities often contained bonfires and feasts, drinking and food. Following on from that were the midsummer celebrations, which likely looked similar to that of the Sumarmál, but few sources document these specific celebrations. But the importance of the midsummer celebrations is illustrated by the fact that the midsummer festivities eventually became St John's Eve in the Christian era, as the Church took over celebrations from the Pagan past.

There were also specific blót sacrifices to certain deities. The Dísablót was a blót sacrifice held in the honour of the Dísir, the goddesses of fate, fertility and family protection. They are often mixed together with other groups such as the Ásynja – female members of the Asir gods; the Norns – the goddesses of fate; the Valkyries – the collector of the fallen; and also, the Fylgja, the familiars or spirits who followed a person or family. This particular feast was possibly originally connected to Freya who is sometimes called 'Vannadís'; this blót was linked to fertility.

Besides these bigger blóts, offerings and rituals took place in the private household. One such example is the Álfablót, held in honour of the álfar (plural: álfar; singular: álfr) or the elves. More on this later. In 'Austrfararvísur', a skaldic poem from 1019 by Sigvat Tordsson, known as Sigvat the Skald, he and his retinue, as Christians, were not welcome and were chased away from the farm when asking for lodging, due to the farmers holding the Álfablót

> Gakkat inn, kvað ekkja,
> armi drengr, in lengra;
> hræðumk ek við Óðins
> (erum heiðin vér) reiði;
> rýgr kvazk inni eiga
> óþekk sús mér hnekði
> alfa blót sem ulfi
> ótvín í bœ sínum.[69]

> 'Do not come any farther in, wretched one', said the woman; 'I fear the anger of Odin'; (we are heathen); the woman who drove me away like a wolf without hesitation, said they held an alfr Blót, inside.

We seem to be informed from the source that it is a woman who is taking care of the sacrifices in this case. As we have seen, this was also the case in the town of Haithabu.

Another example is recorded in *Vǫlsa þáttr* (The Tale of Völsi). Here a horse is butchered and just when the thrall (slave) is about to throw the severed penis of the horse away, the son of the house grabs it and brings it to his mother. She in turn preserves it in herbs and onions and wraps it in a cloth. It is believed to be a phallus symbol and stands for fertility. At the same time, it holds magical properties. Likely there were many other similar rituals that have been lost to us today.

15
Snakes and Serpents in the Norse World

Just as the groves, trees, and water were gateways to the Transcendent, animals were also very important in Scandinavian mythology and beliefs and often involved a shamanistic approach to reaching the Transcendent. Animals, or humans in the shape of animals, held important positions, whether it is the personality of the animal or form they take on, or whether it is the transformation that makes the approach to the Otherworld or the world of the gods possible. But there is no doubt that various animal spirits have an important position in the world of the pre-Christian Germanic area. Even though the sagas written in the Christian era are coloured by the authors' timeframes and beliefs, we can see clear lines when it comes to this. Just as in the Norse belief system animals play a part in upholding the Cosmos, it was also thought that various animals and demons would take part in the destruction of the world at Ragnarök. Such examples include snakes, serpents and/or dragons mentioned in the stories.

As far back as the Bronze Age, snakes have been found engraved on rocks or razor blades, for instance. Snakes are often portrayed as hybrid beings with horse's heads, symbolising fertility.

As an amulet or charm for the treatment of diseases, snake coils are also known from the third period of the Bronze Age, and have been recovered in the Hvidegård find, the Maglehøj find, and a similar find has been made from the Viking Age in Scandinavia, on the Swedish island of Gotland.

Snake iconography dates back to the Bronze Age in Britain as well, which gives the legend surrounding them a long line back in time, perhaps to a common myth believed in both the Celtic and Germanic worlds. The facts illustrate that the beliefs in the beneficial properties of the snake go back centuries.

The mythology and stories from the Viking Age are also full of snakes. Several of the heroes from the sagas of the Viking world, such as Ragnar Lodbrog, fight with snakes/dragons/worms and Ragnar Lodbrog even dies in a snake pit. His son, Sigurd Snake-in-the-Eye, is named after the great dragon slayer Sigurd Fafnerbane.

Under the roots of Yggdrasil, we find several snakes or serpents. One of the most prominent ones is Nidhogg, who gnaws at the tree's roots and is also said to punish those without honour or who are to enter Hel, the Underworld. Other water-dwelling serpents under the roots of Yggdrasil are the serpents Góinn, Grafvitnir, Grafvölludr, Grábakr, Móinn and Sváfnir.

> he stag bites above; | on the side it rotteth,
> And Nídhögg gnaws from below.
> More serpents lie | under Yggdrasill's stock
> Than every unwise ape can think:
> Góinn and Móinn | (they're Grafvitnir's sons),
> Grábakr and Grafvölludr;
> Ófnir and Sváfnir | I think shall aye
> Tear the trunk's twigs.[70]

The names of the dragons or serpents are mentioned in *Skáldskaparmál*. Though sometimes there is a distinction between dragons and serpents, the line is not completely clear. When we look at dragons, they are not the fire-breathing monster we imagine them to be today. Rather they are poisonous and resemble snakes or serpents more than our perception of dragons.

> These are the names of the serpents: Dragon, Fáfnir, mighty monster, Adder, Nídhögg lindworm, she-Adder, Góinn, Móinn, Grafvitnir, Grábakr, Ófnir, Sváfnir, Hooded one.[71]

The mention of the adder is interesting. Soup made from an adder king gives wisdom and knowledge according to Danish folklore. This very king has his own characteristics and magical abilities and stands for wisdom and knowledge; this very knowledge can be passed on to humans.

Then of course we should not forget the giant Jörmungandr, also known as the Midgard Serpent, who dwells in the ocean and encircles the entire world, biting its own tale. The Midgard Serpent is the child of Loki and the giantess, Angrboda. Thor is confronted with the Midgard Serpent twice and according to the myth, Thor will fight the Midgard Serpent in the final battle of Ragnarök.

In *Gylfaginning* Thor is out on a fishing trip. As bait, he uses an oxen head he took from the herd, belonging to the giant Hymir. The Midgard Serpent takes the bait, and they struggled for some time. The giant Hymir became fearful by the sight and cut the fishing line, so Thor's prey slipped away. This very scene is believed to be seen on the runestone from the Hørdum stone in Thy in Denmark.

> The Midgard Serpent snapped at the ox-head, and the hook caught in its jaw; but when the Serpent was aware of this, it dashed away so fiercely that both Thor's fists crashed against the gunwale. Then Thor was angered, and took upon him his divine strength, braced his feet so strongly that he plunged through the ship with both feet, and dashed his feet against the bottom; then he drew the Serpent up to the gunwale. And it may be said that no one has seen very fearful sights who might not see that: now Thor flashed fiery glances at the Serpent, and the Serpent in turn stared up toward him from below and blew venom. Then, it is said, the giant Hymir grew pale, became yellow, and was sore afraid, when he saw the Serpent, and how the sea rushed out and in through the boat. In the very moment when Thor clutched his hammer and raised it on high, then the giant fumbled for his fish-knife and hacked off Thor's line at the gunwale, and the Serpent sank down into the sea. Thor hurled his hammer after it; and men say that he struck off its head against the bottom; but I think it were true to tell thee that the Midgard Serpent yet lives and lies in the encompassing sea. But Thor swung his fist and brought it against Hymir's ear, so that he plunged overboard, and Thor saw the soles of his feet. And Thor waded to land.[72]

Here we have a very good example of the battle between the ordered world in the shape of Thor (a fertility god) and the chaos forces in the shape of the mighty Midgard Serpent. In *Gylfaginning* we are told of Ragnarök and its beginning.

> Then shall happen what seems great tidings: the Wolf shall swallow the sun; and this shall seem to men a great harm. Then the other wolf shall seize the moon, and he also shall work great ruin; the stars shall vanish from the heavens. Then shall come to pass these tidings also: all the earth shall tremble so, and the crags, that trees shall be torn up from the earth, and the crags fall to ruin; and all fetters and bonds shall be broken and rent. Then shall Fenris-Wolf get loose; then the sea shall gush forth upon

> the land, because the Midgard Serpent stirs in giant wrath and advances up onto the land.[73]

The *Gylfaginning* continues:

> The Midgard Serpent shall blow venom so that he shall sprinkle all the air and water; and he is very terrible and shall be on one side of the Wolf.
>
> Thor stands forward on his other side, and can be of no avail to him, because he shall have his hands full fighting against the Midgard Serpent
>
> Thor shall put to death the Midgard Serpent and shall stride away nine paces from that spot; then shall he fall dead to the ground, because of the venom which the Snake has blown at him.

In this tale we have a reference to the number nine: 'He shall stride away nine paces'. When numbers like nine and three are mentioned, it is clear we are deep into myth and the world of magic.

In folklore, it is believed that snakes are able to make you psychic and give you beyond-normal abilities. Saxo's account is from the twelfth and thirteenth centuries and he relates stories from the pre-Christian period. The notion that snakes could be used magically is a very old belief that has continued right up to our modern times. A similar tale can be read in Evald Tang Kristensen, who writes about the folklore of the common people in the nineteenth century. Again, we can see how folk beliefs have long threads, winding back in time.

From the *Gesta Danorum*, Book 6, it is told:

> The father now sent Roller home to see how it was there, and when he saw that there was smoke rising from the house his mother was in, he went there and looked through a little crack and then the mother stood stirring a porridge she cooked in an ugly pot; he also saw three snakes hanging over the pot by a thin string, and that eiders were dripping from their mouths into the porridge; the two were black, the third had a white shell and hung a little higher than the others, for it had the cord in its tail, the others around its belly. He realized that it was some creature of sorcery, and was silent about what he had seen, so as not to get words to accuse his mother of being a Hex; for he did not know

> that the snakes were harmless and how much strength they gave the crop. Regnar and Erik now came, and when they saw the smoke from the cabin, they went straight in and sat down at the table, and Krage set a dish for her son and her stepson so that they could both eat it. The food in it now had a different colour, on one side it was black with yellow spots, and on the other white, which came from the two different kinds of snakes. As soon as they had eaten just a little bit of it, Erik quickly turned the dish so that the black but strong side of the porridge came over to him, and Roller got the white one that had first been set for Erik because this must have realized that with that food it was not the colour, but the power that was in it that mattered; and so that Roller should not notice that there was cunning behind that turning, he said that this is how a ship used to go over the stair when the sea was high, and it was clever enough of him to hide his cunning in that way in that speech about the Ship.
>
> By strengthening himself with this glorious food, Erik, as a consequence of the power that was in it, attained the highest human wisdom; for the fruit was so incredibly strong that it made him knowledgeable in all possible sciences so that he could even interpret what the animals said, for not only did he become thoroughly at home in all human things, but he also understood what the animals meant by the sounds, they gave up, and there he was gifted with such elegant and decorative eloquence that he still, whatever his speech revolved around, adorned it with witty proverbs. since he had achieved the highest degree of intelligence and eloquence at that one hearty meal, and with it the luck of always winning in battle.[74]

In Olaus Magnus' book from 1555, *The History of the Nordic People*, comes a very similar story. It was a general belief that vipers and snakes could drink milk and milk the cows.

> There are also house snakes, which in the far north are considered house gods. They are given cow's and sheep's milk to drink and are often seen sleeping in the cradle as faithful guardians. Harming them is considered sacrilege. These customs, however, are a remnant of ancient superstitions which the Catholic Church has strictly forbidden.[75]

From Buderup parish in the district of Hornum, Denmark, in the eighteenth century:

> On two farms there were many snakes; They were so approachable that they went into the stables and milked the cows, but both families were very prosperous, and therefore no one was allowed to harm the snakes or chase them, otherwise the prosperity would leave the farm.[76]

Here the cows were also milked by the snakes.

In Evald Tang Kristensen's report from the eighteenth century, this can be read:

> A neighbor of ours, whose name was Stine Jakobsen, told us that once as a child she had seen a snake king a stone's throw away from a large standing ditch. It was much larger than the other snakes and had a large golden crown on it. She now did not know what kind of animal it was, and then she ran home to her mother and told her about it. The mother went along, and she could immediately see what it was.
>
> She then said that they mustn't harm it, because then they would get all the other snakes after them.
>
> From Fyen. Andreas Jensen, Vonsild.

The notion that the snake should not be disturbed is reminiscent of the notion one had around the burial mounds where the Otherworldly lived. If you touched them or did damage to them, you would have bad luck.

> In Køge – were snakes and you didn't do anything to them because you thought they were lucky. (West Zealand.)

If you could capture a viper king and boil its fat, you could become psychic:

> There was a karl who had read in Cyprian how to lure a Viper King to him. He also gets hold of one and gives it to his mother to see if she would cook it for him, because whoever eats the fat of a viper king can become psychic and can see just as well what is inside as outside, and just as well what is many miles away as what is near.

> She did so, but the Work hand had gone outside in the meantime because that is how it was prescribed.
>
> There was a girl on the farm, and she was curious to know what adder fat tasted like, and so she got up to skim some of the pot with a spoon and ate it. Then she went out to milk.
>
> However, the fellow also ate some of the fat, but he did not notice any change in his vision, for it is only the first spoonful that had power.
>
> He had an errand over in the emergency, and when he got there, the girl said:
>
> 'What a big, red-coloured bull calf there is in our helmeted cow.'
>
> Now the man could understand where the knowledge had gone because the cow had a calf like that.

In Jens Kamps' *Dansk Folketro*, you can read that in order to protect clothes from moths and worms, you must take a viper's skin (the discarded viper's skin that is most often found on the heath) and put it between the clothes.

In the same place, this is told from West Zealand:

> Just as there is a viper king, there is also a snake king: It has a crown on its head and a mane – Whoever can catch it, have it cooked and eat the soup, becomes psychic. Can see the calf in the cow, the child in the mother's womb and can also see seven cubits into the ground (West Zealand).[77]

Here is exactly the same idea that we read about in Saxo's account in the *Gesta Danorum*. Many men and women are later said to have worked as a wise man or woman after eating the fat from a snake or viper.

> And the girl, it was none other than her, they later called the wise woman.
>
> Sigurd J. Kristensen.

In a tale from Jutland, we hear that 'in case of cattle disease, a live viper is placed in a pot or a bottle and buried inside or outside the door of the barn. This remedy was used for diseases of livestock. Which also meant it was protected against witchcraft'.

Sometimes in newly built houses, it was also custom to bury a live viper; the same goes for getting good crops:

> Some folklore has been attached to Snakes and Worms. Vipers that were caught before May Day and buried in the farmyard, warded off witchcraft.[78]

It is clear in the many tales that the belief in the magical abilities of snakes was widespread in the pre-Christian world and in mythology. It was a belief that the Church tried to eradicate, but it continued unimpeded.

A bronze razor found on the Vestrup field has been dated to the Bronze Age, and details we see displayed on both rock carvings and bronze objects give us a good idea of the religious beliefs that the people held then.

> Furthermore, a new interpretation of the connection between the central anthropomorphic, a supposed woman, and the snake-like animal is put forward. It is suggested that the woman in a line or cord holds a bowl – what has previously been interpreted as a snake's head. A snake – three undulating lines narrowing at one end – drinks from the bowl.

On the Sutton Hoo helmet, besides dancing warriors we also find three dragon/serpent heads. The iconography shows a link to Scandinavia and the Germanic beliefs prior to Christianity. A detectorist found a little stamp on the island of Tåsinge in Denmark with iconography similar to the Sutton Hoo helmet, pointing to the helmet possibly being crafted in Denmark instead of Sweden as previously believed. Since the Jutes and Angels came from an area in close proximity to that of the Danes, this would make sense. As shown with DNA research on the Viking world, the Danes went west to England and France, as the Swedes went east.

Snakes in English folklore often merge with dragon legends, featuring giant serpents known as 'worms', such as the Lambton Worm, that terrorise villages. As in Danish, worm/wyrm in old middle English in the medieval era often means a snake or dragon. The Lambton Worm is a famous folk tale from the River Wear in County Durham. According to legend, the local heir, John, skips church on a Sunday to go fishing. Here he catches an ugly 'worm' which he later throws into a well. He then leaves for the Holy Land on Crusade, while the ugly worm grows large and becomes a pestilence to the area. John receives advice from a local wise woman and he must swear an oath:

> John thanked her. He was turning to go when she called him back. 'One thing more,' said the Wise Woman. 'If thou kill the worm, thou must swear a vow. The first living thing that meets thee as

> thou crossest the threshold of Lambton Hall – *that thing thou must put to death.* Break this vow and for nine generations, no Lambton shall die in his bed.
> John shuddered. But he swore the oath.[79]

The first person John meets after he has killed the worm is his very own father.

> The worm was gone. The land was safe. The people cheered. But the vow had been broken – for John had meant to kill Boris first, and instead his father had reached him first. And for nine generations, none of the Lambtons died peacefully in his bed. The very last of that cursed line, it is said, died in his carriage one dark afternoon, crossing the bridge at Brugeford.

Here we have a classic folklore tale with number nine as part of the story. This very story of the worm growing proportionally large has similarities with the story we find of Ragnar Lodbrog, who gains his nickname by battling a large 'Worm' snake that has grown so proportionally large that no one can reach his future wife, Thora. Similar stories are told of the 'Lind Worm' in Danish folklore. In this tale, it grows so large that it curls itself around a church. It was also said to have a liking to eat beautiful virgins.

Another such serpent from English folklore is the Sussex Serpent; a documented report in a 1614 pamphlet describes a 9-foot serpent with a black back and red belly in Sussex, which allegedly killed people and dogs with venom.

Yet again we have the 'worm' or dragon who behaves more like a snake than a dragon, and spewing poison instead of fire, just like the Midgard Worm does when he kills Thor.

Whether these stories are from the Anglo-Saxon period prior to the Viking Age is hard to say. When looking at the Sutton Hoo grave iconography, it suggests an older tradition that that of the Vikings, more likely coming from the Angels, Saxons and the Jutes whose beliefs were similar to that of the Norse.

The fossilised remains of ammonites were given the name snakestones in England because they resemble coiled snakes turned to stone. These fossils are often associated with the small town of Whitby in Yorkshire, and Whitby was a place that had a Viking heritage. According to legend, Saint Hilda turned all snakes to stone since snakes in Christian beliefs have a poor standing. This legend is supposedly from the seventh century, so could originate from the Anglo-Saxon era, and therefore root to a more common Germanic tradition.

Another legend concerning dragons is the legend of St George, who replaced Edward the Confessor as the patron saint of England. The story features Dragon Hill near the Uffington White horse where, reputedly, it is said here that green grass never grows where the dragon blood was spilled. The story gained traction as one of the stories that the Crusaders brought home with them from the holy land and is a blend of myth, legend and medieval history.

In the folklore of Herefordshire, you can read about the dragon's well:

> The Church at Brinsop is dedicated to St George, and contains a fine tympanum of eleventh century date, representing St George mounted, in the act of slaying the dragon. The dragon's well is in Duck's pool meadow, on the south side of the church, while on the other side is a field called 'Lower Stanks' pointing out by the parish clerk as the spot where St George slew the dragon.[80]

16

The Horse in the Norse World

Another animal with a central place in the Norse world is the horse. Often mentioned by name in the sagas, the horse's important function is to uphold the Cosmos. In Sturluson's *Younger Edda*, the list of named horses is very long.

In *Gylfaginning*, we also hear of the horses of the Aesir:

> Each day the Aesir ride thither up over Bifröst, which is also called the Aesir's Bridge. These are the names of the Aesir's steeds: Sleipnir is best, which Odin has; he has eight feet. The second is Gladr, the third Gyllir, the fourth Glenr, the fifth Skeidbrimir, the sixth Silfrintoppr, the seventh Sinir, the eighth Gisl, the ninth Falhófnir, the tenth. Gulltoppr, the eleventh Léttfeti. Baldr's horse was burnt with him, and Thor walks to the judgment, and wades those rivers which are called thus.[81]

One of the best-known horses is of course Odin's eight-legged horse Sleipnir, who is mentioned several times, in *Gylfaginning*, *Skáldskaparmál* and elsewhere. According to the story in *Gylfaginning*, Sleipnir is the child of Loki, when he took the shape of a mare, and the stallion Svadilfari.

> That same evening, when the wright drove out after stone with the stallion Svadilfari, a mare bounded forth from a certain wood and called to him. The stallion, perceiving what manner of horse this was, straightway became frantic, and snapped the traces asunder, and leapt over to the mare, and she went away to the wood, and the wright after, striving to seize the stallion.[82]

In the transformation or shapeshifting of Loki, he ends up giving birth to the eight-legged horse Sleipnir as further described in *Gylfaginning*:

> But Loki had such dealings with Svadilfari, that somewhat later he gave birth to a foal, which was grey and had eight feet; and this horse is the best among gods and men.
>
> The sun or the sun wagon is pulled across the sky by the two horses Alsvinn and Arvak. Arvak means 'early riser' and Alsvinn 'All Swifts or very quick'.[83]

Arvak and Alsvinn are also mentioned in *Gylfaginning* and *Grímnismál*. This is from the *Grímnismál*:

> Arvak and Alsvinn
> Up shall drag,
> Weary the weight of the sun,
> But an iron cool,
> Have the kindly Gods,
> Of Yore set under their yokes.[84]

What iron cool means is debated, but what is clear is that the intention of it was to protect the horses from the heat of the sun.

Two other horses, Skinfaxi and Hrimfaxi are also connected to the Cosmos. Skinfaxi means 'shining mane' and Hrimfaxi, 'frost mane'. They are the horses belonging to Dagr (day) and Nótt (night). In *Gylfaginning* this can be read:

> Nörfi or Narfi is the name of a giant that dwelt in Jötunheim: he had a daughter called Night; she was swarthy and dark, as befitted her race. She was given to a man named Naglfari; their son was Audr. Afterwards, she was wedded to him which was called Annarr; Jörd was their daughter. Last of all Dayspring had her, and he was of the race of the Aesir; their son was Day: he was radiant and fair after his father. Then All father took Night, and Day her son, and gave to them two horses and two chariots, and sent them up into the heavens, to ride round about the earth every two half-days. Night rides before with the horse named Frosty-Mane, and on each morning, he bedews the earth with the foam from his bit. The horse that Day has is called Sheen-Mane, and he illumines all the air and the earth from his mane.[85]

The story of a horse taking the sun and moon across the sky is very old. A sun wagon was found in a bog at Trundholm in Denmark and dated to about 1400 BC. It shows a sun disk placed on a wagon pulled by a horse. Of course, we cannot say if the Bronze Age sun wagon or the story behind it is the same as that from the *Younger Edda* but there is no doubt that the horse up through time has had this prominent position in myth.

The importance of the horse as both a religious and a high-status symbol is seen also in graves. High-status graves are found with horses sacrificed as part of the funeral rite. One such is the Ladby Ship Burial on the island of Funen in Denmark. Here as many as eleven horses were placed in the grave with the king, emphasising the importance of the horse.

Alongside that, we have horse skulls buried inside walls or under floors of buildings up through time and into the Christian era. This was believed to give protection against sorcery. We still see this tradition in folklore all the way up to the modern day. The skull of a horse was often placed near the entrances of houses such as doors, windows, or the fireplace. This was often also the case with the entrance to a stable, where the corpse of a dog or a live snake in a bottle could also be buried as a sacrifice to protect against evil sorcery.

That the horse was connected to myth and magic is also seen in the story of the 'Nidpole'. Nio means to mock or taunt. Nidding (modern Danish) is a person without honour. The Nidpole is mentioned in *Egil's Saga*:

> And when all was ready for sailing, Egil went up onto the island. He took in his hand a hazel-pole and went to a rocky eminence that looked inward to the mainland. Then he took a horse's head and fixed it on the pole. After that, in solemn form of the curse, he thus spake: 'Here set I up a curse-pole, and this curse I turn on King Eric and Queen Gunnhilda. This curse I turn also on the guardian-spirits who dwell in this land, that they may all wander astray, nor reach or find their home till they have driven out of the land King Eric and Gunnhilda.' This spoken, he planted the pole down in a rift of the rock and let it stand there. The horse's head he turned inwards to the mainland; but on the pole he cut runes, expressing the whole form of curse.[86]

A 'Nidding' pole or 'Nid' pole was made of hazel, with a freshly cut horse's head on the top; the pole was to be pointed in the direction of the one you wanted to curse. Hazel is generally believed to have magical properties. This is the case in both Norse and Celtic tradition and is seen in later folklore as well. In many cultures, hazel is thought to give inspiration and wisdom. Traditionally, it was thought to protect you from lightning and against sorcery of various kinds, including against the Otherworldly beings. In this case the Nidpole was carved with runes.

A survey of horses in Viking Age Scandinavia shows that eighteen out of nineteen horses in graves were stallions. Yggdrasil, as mentioned previously, means Odin's horse. In the fourteenth-century *Flateyjarbók* we hear of a ritual concerning a preserved horse's penis. The ritual's purpose was fertility and hence hoping to secure the wealth of the farm. This demonstrates that the gender of the animal was also significant in the beliefs, as seemingly only stallions were useful in these rites.

According to folklore in Denmark a Hel-horse is a church grim (a guardian spirit) who was buried alive as a sacrifice so that the church could be built. In Danish they were called 'kirkevarer' meaning church omen, and if this ghostly horse was seen it was to warn you against imminent death.

17

Wolves in the Norse World

The wolf has several meanings in Norse myth. Odin had two wolves, Geri and Freki, Geri meaning the greedy one and Freki meaning the gluttonous one. They sit at Odin's feet and follow him into battle. Odin feeds them food while he himself drinks wine.

> Geri and Freki the war-wont sates,
> the triumphant sire of hosts;
> but on wine only the famed in arms,
> Odin, ever lives.

In 'Helgakvida Hunningsbana I', we are told that they roam the battlefield, eager to consume the corpses of the fallen.

> The warriors went to the trysting place of swords,
> which they had appointed at Logafiöll.
> Broken was Frodi's peace between the foes:
> Vidrir's hounds went about the isle slaughter-greedy.[87]

The Frodi's peace or 'Frodefred' is broken. As discussed, earlier Frode was a Danish king that upheld peace in his realm.

The sun and moon were said to be hunted by two wolves – Skoll (the one who mocks) and Hati (the one who hates). At Ragnarök, they finally catch up with their prey and devour the sun and moon. From *Grímnismál*:

> Skoll is the name of the wolf
> Who follows the shining priest
> Into the desolate forest,
> And the other is Hati,

Hródvitnir's son,
Who chases the bright bride of the sky.[88]

In *The Völuspa* we hear of the giantess who sits in Ironwood. Ironwood is a place inhabited by a troll woman who gives birth to wolves and Jötnar.

The giantess old in Ironwood sat,
In the east, and bore the brood of Fenrir:
Among these one in monster's guise
Was soon to steal the sun from the sky.

Fenrir himself is to have a great part in the destruction of the world at Ragnarök. It's siblings are the Midgard Serpent (or Jörmungandr), and Hel that rules over the Underworld. In one version of the myth, it is in fact Fenrir that will devour the sun at Ragnarök.

Much I have travelled, much have I tried out,
much have I tested the Powers;
from where a sun will come into the smooth heaven
when Fenrir has assailed this one?[89]

Fenrir is also to devour Odin at Ragnarök according to *The Völuspa.*

Then is fulfilled Odin's
Second sorrow,
When Odin goes
To fight with the wolf,
And Beli's slayer
Bright, against surtr.
Sweet friend fall.[90]

In *Gylfaginning*, the wolves that hunt the sun are also mentioned:

'Then' said Gangleri, 'The sun fares swiftly, and almost as if she were afraid: she could not hasten her course any the more if she feared her destruction'. Then Hárr made answer: 'It is no marvel that she hastens furiously; close cometh he that seeks her, and she has no escape save to run away'. Then said Gangleri, 'Who is he that causes her this disquiet?' Hárr replied: 'It is two wolves; and

> he that runs after her is called Skoll; she fears him, and he shall take her. But he that leaps before her is called Hati Hródvitnisson. He is eager to seize the moon; and so, it must be'.[91]

In the same place we are also told where all the wolves come from.

> 'Wolves?' Hárr answered, 'A witch dwells to the east of Midgard, in the forest called Ironwood: in that wood dwell the troll-women, who are known as Ironwood-Women. The old witch bears many giants for sons, and all in the shape of wolves; and from this source are these wolves sprung'.

Troll women, witches and Jötnar are synonymous of the chaos forces – powers that are out of control. The gods maintain the order of things and anything that lives outside of the ordered world, in Utgaard, are the powers of chaos. These powers will, in the end, destroy the world.

In *Gylfaginning*, we are told that the wolves will swallow the sun and the moon and bring about the destruction of the ordered Cosmos:

> Then shall happen what seems great tidings: the Wolf shall swallow the sun; and this shall seem to men a great harm. Then the other wolf shall seize the moon, and he also shall work great ruin; the stars shall vanish from the heavens.[92]

Iconography from the Iron Age and the Viking Age illustrates that animal masks, animal shapes, and shapeshifting were all part of the beliefs and rituals. Thus, we find on the Golden Horns of Gallehus, a pair of fifth-century horns discovered in Denmark, an array of pictures with religious context and ritualistic procession depicting animal masks or perhaps shapeshifters. Perhaps these pictures speak of the famed Ulfhednar and Berserkers, elite warriors dedicated to Odin. The word berserk is used today for a person who goes crazy. Back in the Viking Age, the berserkers and Ulfhednar were warriors that were said to fight in a sort of rage or frenzy. Some think they fought naked, foaming at the mouth and even biting their own shields. I believe these special warriors were ritualistically initiated into a group of people, taking on the mindset of an animal such as the wolf or the bear. Perhaps this was in some way connected to the concept of 'sitting out' (in Old Norse 'útiseta' or 'udsidning') which is an ancient Nordic magical practice originating from the Viking Age and Norse beliefs. It is a form of seidr (magic) or shamanistic ritual practice in which a person sits alone in nature, often at night, to make contact with supernatural beings, gods, ancestors, or spirits. In that way it may also have been connected to the Fylgja. The Fylgja supposedly reflected the personality of the person it was connected too; hence a temperamental person or strong person could have a Fylgja such as the wolf or the bear.

When it comes to werewolves in English folklore it seems there is a lack of stories. Sabine Baring-Gould, a nineteenth-century scholar, believes that it is because wolves were no longer perceived as a threat by the Anglo-Saxon period, yet the term Werwulf (meaning man dog) existed in old English, pointing to old legends of the term. The Flixton Werewolf, often nicknamed 'Old Stinker', is a legendary, hair-covered wolf or dog with a terrible stench and glowing red eyes said to roam the countryside near Flixton, North Yorkshire, since AD 940. Since Yorkshire was part of the Danelaw, this story could easily stem from Norse lore.

According to Danish folklore, you would become a werewolf through a curse:

> Now at the time when there were werewolves. My father himself did not see it, but he heard it from his father, and he heard it from an old man in Magleby, and he himself saw it.
>
> There was this man in Magleby, he came riding out towards the forest one evening, and then he saw 10 or 11 girls who had stretched out a foal skin (with a hole in it) and the three of them had jumped through it. He thought it was wrong, rode up and chased them all with his whip right in front of him, back to the town and right through the town, and they were all quite naked.

This ritual is also mentioned in *Sagn og historier fra København og omegn.* (Folklore and history from the area of Copenhagen and surrounding area), which adds how this curse works.

> The baker said that it was the mothers' fault that their children turned into werewolves. For if a fertile woman crawled through a horse's skin to escape the pains of childbirth, the child she gave birth to becomes a poor animal; if it was a boy, he became a werewolf, if it was a girl, a mare.

It was thought that women would be free from pain when they were about to give birth if they crawled naked through a hole in a colt's skin. But if a woman undertook this ritual, her child would become a werewolf if a boy and a mare if a girl. The mare (Old English, maere; Norse, mara) is also a mythological being from Norse myth and is portrayed as a female creature that rides on a human's chest when they sleep, giving them chest tightness and bad dreams. Hence the word 'nightmare'; in Danish 'mareridt'. The first literary mention of a mara is in Snorri Sturluson's *Ynglinga Saga* from the thirteenth century; the story itself takes place in the ninth century. The custom is likely a garbled version of a ritual from the pre-Christian era.

Werewolves were also said to pursue pregnant women, since they had to devour an unborn child to break the curse. According to legend, the werewolves would gang up on pregnant women and tear her to pieces to be freed from the witchcraft.

Another far more benign way of being freed from the curse was for someone to say out loud 'You are a werewolf'.

> A man and a woman were driving along the road. Then it occurred to him that he should go for a walk.
>
> 'Now I'm going,' he said, 'and you stay by the cart; and if anyone comes and attacks you, you must use nothing but this red mat, which I give you to defend yourself with'.
>
> Sometime after the man had gone, a black dog came and wanted to get into the cart with her, and it seemed to want to do her harm. She defended herself as best she could with the mat, and the dog bit it several times, but when the fight had lasted a while, it ran away.
>
> A short time later, the man came back.
>
> 'It's good that you're coming,' she said, and she told him about the dog and the fight that had taken place between them. As they drove on, she discovered that the man had red threads between his teeth.
>
> 'Huh, it's you who's been here,' she said.
>
> 'Yes, thank you for fighting so bravely, now I am saved from that plague for the future.'
>
> Kristian Andersen, Kjertinge.[93]

Defending yourself with an apron is a common theme. The werewolf would often take part in breaking the curse by advising the woman to defend herself with an apron; she would recognise him when he was back to his human shape by seeing shreds of the apron between his teeth.

A werewolf walking on three legs or only having three legs is another typical part of the stories. We see this also in stories of witches transformed into hares;

a person who has shapeshifted also sometimes run on three legs. The number three is central in folklore and is highly connected to sorcery.

> My father has told me that he has seen a werewolf. One evening, he went out to take care of his own business (on his own errand) and sat down in the mud. Then he saw at once such a hideous one, like a big ugly dog, coming and biting him. It had only three legs. My father then took a fence post and hit what one would now call the back end, and then it ran away again.
>
> But a few days later, there was a party in the town, and then the person about whom they said it was a werewolf walked and limped, and it looked on his legs as if he had been hit by a post.
>
> The next day, when it was the second day of the wedding, my father went behind the farm, and then the werewolf came after him again. But my father always had a post with him, with which he hit him, and then he ran away.
>
> The man who was blamed for being a werewolf was such a strange little fellow with a big head, and his wife said that he always went away at a certain time of the night.

That the transformation happens at night is not a new idea. We see something similar in the saga of Kveldulf's son:

> Egil's grandfather was named Ulf; he lived in the Fjords region of Norway, where he held the office of sheriff, just as his ancestors had before him. He was an industrious husbandman and a good advisor to those who sought his advice. But every day, as evening approached, he became sleepy and shy. Many believed that his soul, when sleep came over him, took up residence in a wolf's den. For this reason, he was called Kveldulf.

That the transformation happened at night or in a trance-like state was a common theme in the old stories. This is also mentioned The *Ynglinga Saga* by Snorri Sturluson, in connection with Odin.

> Óðinn skipti hömum; lá þá búkrinn sem sofinn eða dauðr, en hann var þá fugl eða dýr, fiskr eða ormr, ok fór á einni svipstund á fjarlæg lönd, at sínum erendum eða annarra manna.

Odin could transform his shape: his body would lie as if dead, or asleep; but then he would be in the shape of a fish, or worm, or bird, or beast, and be off in a twinkling to distant lands upon his own or other people's business.

18

Boars, Hogs, and Pigs in Norse Mythology

Pigs and hogs also have an important role in Norse mythology. The god Frey had a boar called Gullinbursti. Frey was heavily connected to boars and sacrifices of boars or swine were made to him. Gullinbursti's creation is related in *Skáldskaparmál*.

> Sindri laid a pigskin in the hearth and bade Brokkr blow and did not cease work until he took out of the hearth that which he had laid therein. But when he went out of the smithy, while the other dwarf was blowing, straightway a fly settled upon his hand and stung yet he blew on as before, until the smith took the work out of the hearth; and it was a boar, with mane and bristles of gold. Then Brokkr brought forward his gifts: ... to Freyr he gave the boar, saying that it could run through air and water better than any horse, and it could never become so dark with night or gloom of the Murky Regions that there should not be sufficient light where he went, such was the glow from its mane and bristles.[94]

In the story of the death of Baldr, the most beautiful of the gods and the son of Odin and Frigg, the blind god Höd is deceived by Loki, and ends up killing Baldr (Balder) by striking him with mistletoe. Baldr's mother had taken all other plants into oath so they could not hurt him, except for one little plant of mistletoe. She had forgotten or thought the plant to be too insignificant, thinking she did not need too. Baldr was the god of justice.

In the skaldic poem of Húsdrápá we find Frey riding on Gullinbursti to the funeral of Baldr. Húsdrápá is also preserved partially in *The Younger Edda*.

> On the boar with golden bristles
> rode the God Frey battle wise

Odin and his ravens. (Anette Guldager Boye)

Geri and Freki, Odin’s wolves. (Anette Guldager Boye)

Hati who devours the moon. (Anette Guldager Boye)

A Berserker. (Anette Guldager Boye)

Right: Thor on a fishing trip. (Anette Guldager Boye)

Below: Serimnir and Heidrun with Odin. (Anette Guldager Boye)

The wild hunt. (Anette Guldager Boye)

Light men. (Anette Guldager Boye)

Above: Brownies and Nisse. (Anette Guldager Boye)

Right: Fairies dancing in a fairy ring. (Anette Guldager Boye)

The Lind Worm, a serpent-like creature. (Anette Guldager Boye)

Lone mermaid. (Anette Guldager Boye)

Selkie. (Anette Guldager Boye)

Tower of London. (Anette Guldager Boye)

Black Shuck. (Anette Guldager Boye)

Kelpie. (Anette Guldager Boye)

> to arrange the following, where Odin's
> young Son was to be burned.[95]

In *Gylfaginning* he is riding a chariot with Gullinbursti pulling the chariot.

Frey's twin sister, Freya, also has a boar, called Hildisvini. The name of the boar means battle swine. Hildisvini appears in a story where Freya is searching for the ancestry of Ottár, her protégé, only to find out that Hildisvini is really Ottár in disguise. In the tale, they meet with Hyndla, who is a seeress, to aid them in their quest.

In Valhöll we also have the pig Sæhrímnir who is killed and cooked every day to feed the gods and the Einherjar – the fallen warriors of Valhöll/Valhalla. Sæhrimnír is like Thor's two goats Tanngrisnir and Tanngnjóstr, in that he becomes whole again the next day.

> 'Then' said Gangleri: 'Thou sayest that all those men who have fallen in battle from the beginning of the world are now come to Odin in Valhall. What has he to give them for food? I should think that a very great host must be there.' Then Hárr answered: 'That which thou sayest is true: a very mighty multitude is there, but many more shall be, notwithstanding which it will seem all too small, in the time when the Wolf shall come. But never is so vast a multitude in Valhall that the flesh of that boar shall fail, which is called Sæhrímnir; he is boiled every day and is whole at evening. But this question which thou askest now: I think it is likelier that few may be so wise as to be able to report truthfully concerning it. His name who roasts is Andhrímnir, and the kettle is Eldhrímnir; so, it is said here:
>
> Andhrímnir | has in Eldhrímnir.
> Sæhrímnir sodden,
> Best of hams; | yet how few know
> With what food the champions are fed.'[96]

The pig was also utilised on the household farm as well as symbolically and interwoven in myth. In Saxo's *Gesta Danorum: History of the Danes* we are told of the Battle of Bravalla. In this battle the old Danish king of the Scyldings, Harald 'Hildetand', also known as Harald War Tooth, fought against the supposed father of Ragnar Lodbrog, Sigurd Ring. Sigurd had previously been made king of Sweden by his uncle, none other than Harald War Tooth.

In this battle Odin intervenes personally. One of the battle formations consists of one resembling a boar's head. In Saxo's account, Odin is advising Sigurd Ring in this very formation. Harald becomes suspicious of what he is being told and realises that the battle had taken a poor turn for the Danes because his opponents have also learned this very formation. (Brun is Odin in disguise.)

> Brun's face relaxed into something of a smile, and he answered that he was fighting with a line in the form of a wedge. When the king heard this, he began to be alarmed, and to ask in great astonishment from whom Ring could have learnt this method of disposing his line, especially as Odin was the discoverer and imparter of this teaching.[97]

This Svinfylking or 'Boars snout' was a military formation used in the Iron Age in Scandinavia and the Germanic lands and was known as 'Schweinskopf' or 'Swine's Head'. The invention of the formation is attributed to Odin and would likely have been known to the Anglo-Saxons as well. Iron Age helmets with the motif of boars have been discovered by archaeologists. These are especially seen in Denmark, Sweden, and the Anglo-Saxon areas. On the Torslunda plates from the Island of Öland, Sweden, we are presented with a depiction of warriors carrying boars' heads.

The Anglo-Saxon Benty Grange helmet, discovered in Derbyshire in 1848 and originating from the seventh century, carries a boar's crest which faces a cross, thus displaying a mixture of Pagan and Christian iconography. This is a good indication of a slow conversion to Christianity, keeping some of the old traditions and myth in place while adapting to a new faith. As beliefs transitioned, it is not unusual to see this mixture, before a full conversion has taken place. Since the boar was also emblematic of battle as we have seen, the boar crest would also have been associated with protection. Further, the Christian cross was often used as an extra talisman in the Norse and Germanic areas even by those not fully converted to the Christian beliefs.

Boar-crested helmets are also mentioned in *Beowulf* although whether or not the poem belongs to the Anglo-Saxon period has been partially disputed. The historian Richard North argues that part of the manuscript was written in England after the Danish Cnut became king of England in 1016. But the present writer is inclined to think most of the poem is built on a longer oral tradition. New parts might have been 'turned' to legitimise Cnut's claim to the Danish throne, laying his claim as a descendant of the Scylding line. This, however, does not mean the story laid out did not exist beforehand. The author who wrote it down might just have added or changed some details to fit the narrative. Since we have indications of the boar formation from archaeology in the Iron Age, a lot points to this.

Another example is the Guilden Morden Boar which was found in 1884 in Cambridgeshire. It is from the sixth or seventh century and believed to have been attached to a helmet at some point, which yet again points to the importance of the boar in myth and legend.

It was also traditional to swear or make an oath by laying hands on the Sónargöltr (the sacrificial pig slaughtered at Christmas). This tradition is known from the *Hervarar Saga*, *Heiðarvíga Saga* and *Pål-Saga* (*Hálfdanar saga Skatala*), where placing your hand on the brushes of the pig and swearing an oath would give a promise of great accomplishment in the future.

19

Goats in Norse Mythology

Tanngrisnir and Tanngnjóstr are the goats of Thor and likely those most known from Norse mythology. Tanngrisnir translates to 'teeth-barer, or snarler' and Tanngnjóstr to 'teeth-grinder'. How the names of the goats are written varies a little, but the translation of the names is close. In *Gylfaginning* we are presented with a description of Thor plus a mention of his goats. The fact that Thor can sacrifice his goats and resurrect them again afterwards, places him as a fertility god.

> Thor has two he-goats, that are called Tooth-Gnasher and Tooth-Gritter, and a chariot wherein he drives, and the he-goats draw the chariot; therefore, is he called Öku-Thor.[98]

In one of the myths, Thor is out travelling to the lodging of a human farmer and his family. Thor slaughters his goats and shares the meal with the family. The family's son splits the bone of one of the goats for the marrow.

> Öku-Thor drove forth with his he-goats and chariot, and with him that Ás called Loki; they came at evening to a husbandman, and there received a night's lodging. About in the evening, Thor took his he-goats and slaughtered them both; after that they were flayed and born to the caldron. When the cooking was done, Thor and his companion sat down for supper. Thor invited to meet with him the husbandman and his wife, and their children: the husbandman's son was called Thjálfi, and the daughter Röskva. Then Thor laid the goat-hides farther away from the fire and said that the husbandman and his servants should cast the bones on the goat-hides. Thjálfi, the husbandman's son, was holding a thighbone of the goat, and split it with his knife and broke it for the marrow.[99]

These very goats can be killed, eaten, and then resurrected by Thor the next day. However, the boy, Thjálfi, had split the bone, making one of the goats lame. Of course, Thor is mighty upset by this but calms down when he sees how frightened the farmer and his family are. In the end the two children, the boy Thjálfi and the girl Röskva, become Thor's servants.

Another goat named and of significance in Norse mythology is the goat Heiðrún or Heidrun which gives forth mead to be served in Valhöll to the Einherjar, the fallen of Valhöll/Valhalla.

> A goat called Heiðrún stands up [on its hind-legs] in Valhalla biting the buds off the branches of that very famous tree which is called Læráth. From her teats runs the mead with which every day she fills a cauldron, which is so big that all the Einherjar can drink their fill from it.[100]

As described by the Skalds, the mead is connected to knowledge and wisdom and is called the drink of the Gods. This renders this goat significant as it produces the very drink of knowledge and Skaldmanship.

In English folklore, goats are typically linked to the devil due to their horns and hooves. According to *The Denham Tracts*, keeping a goat at an inn or a farm would bring the owner good luck. It would also bring good health to the other animals at the farm. *The Denham Tracts* were a series of folklore pamphlets collected between 1846–1859 by Michael Aislabie Denham, a tradesman from Yorkshire. Once again we can see how a Norse myth, given that Yorkshire was an area that was the centre of Danelaw, can travel down through the centuries and become part of the fabric of English folklore. Thor's goats were seen as a symbol of fertility and good luck, hence why here in Yorkshire goats were considered to be bringers of good luck rather than being associated with the devil.

20

Shapeshifting

The Old Norse phrase denoting the process of shapeshifting is *skipta hömum*, 'to change shape' and being able to change shape is called '*hamramr*' (having a strong '*hamramr*'). Certain people were believed to have the ability to change 'hamr' shape, especially those involved in sorcery.

Perhaps some of the most well-known shapeshifters come from the Germanic world, where we find the Ulfhednar and Berserkers, elite warriors of Odin who were thought to be able to shapeshift into bears and wolves. Kings often had Berserkers in their army and in reality they were likely elite warriors clad in wolf or bearskin, who entered such a state of mind that they fought in a frenzy. Odin was known as the god of frenzy and Adam of Bremen explicitly associates Odin with the Latin term furore, which can be translated as 'rage', 'fury', 'madnesses, or 'frenzy' – Wotan [Odin] id est furore. The stories tell us of these men who fought with the strength of a bear or a wolf.

Today, to go berserk is synonymous with running amok or being completely out of control. This makes sense given that the word berserk refers to a particular form of combat practiced in the Viking Age, in which the fighters threw off their chainmail and tunics and fought naked. Filled with rage and without fear for his own life, the Berserker cast himself into the midst of the battle arousing terror amongst friends and foes alike. They were even known to bite their own shields out of pure rage.

Interestingly, a chess piece was found carved out of a walrus tooth at a Nordic workshop from the second half of the 1100s. It served as a player in a set of chess pieces and is one of the seventy-eight pieces found in 1831 on the Isle of Lewis, Hebrides. Here the figure bites its shield, so there is no doubt that the concept of going berserk was known before the stories were written down about these fearsome warriors. Several of the sagas inform us about Berserkers, and how kings and earls deployed them in their armies.[101]

These shapeshifting warriors are often portrayed as naked or semi-naked men, one of the most famous depictions being on the Golden Horns from Gallehus, originating from the Iron Age around AD 400. Here they are pictured with weapons, shields and horned helmets. The term 'horned helmets' is perhaps not quite what people would think. On the Island of Funen, in Denmark, a figure from the eighth century was found in 2016. The figurine is five centimetres tall and is believed to show Odin. The horns on his helmet are actually two birds that represent Odin's two ravens, Hugin and Mugin. A similar figurine, with less damage, was found at Tissø, and here we can clearly see the birds. Very few of these kinds of figures are found in Scandinavia, but others have been found with similar headgear, and depictions of the Gallehus Golden Horns bear resemblance to this figurine.

This can be read in a Danish article. The information is from the East Funish Museum:

> It is not horns that the figure has on the helmet, but rather two birds. It is most likely a representation of or a symbol for Odin's two companions, the ravens Hugin and Munin. We know such costume pins with helmeted or bird-carrying warriors from several special and rich Viking sites, including Tissø in West Zealand, Uppåkra in Scania and Staraja Ladoga in Russia, to name just a few. On several of the other finds, the tips of the horns end in bird heads – but on the figure from Mesinge, the tips may have broken off, explains Malene Refshauge.[102]

The golden horns illustrate a religious ritual; with the warriors or Berserkers placed in this same religious sphere there is a strong likelihood that Berserkers were involved in some sort of shamanistic initiation where they perhaps were to live as a bear or wolf.

The exact translation of Berserker has long been debated. For a long time it was thought it meant bare shirt, hence fighting naked in a frenzy. But others think it could possibly mean Bear shirt – the man gaining the strength of the bear.

Berserkers were not just employed by kings – kings themselves could also be Berserkers. One story tells of the legendary Berserker and Danish king, Angantyr, and his eleven brothers, all who were Berserkers. Angantyr carried the enchanted sword Tyrfing, a sword, given to him by his father, that bestowed endless power and eternal victory on the battlefield, but with it came a curse of eternal perdition to the owner and his family. The sword could not be drawn and put back without it tasting blood. Angantyr constructed a gigantic canal, which bore across the island of Samsø, and was called the Kanhave Canal. With it in place, Angantyr could place his dragon fleets in Stavns Fjord, from where it could easily move from one part of the Danish kingdom to the other. Angantyr and his eleven brothers supposedly died at a battle on Samsø. The story of Angantyr is mentioned in the *Hervor Saga* and *Gesta Danorum: A History of the Danes*. In the *Hervor Saga*, Angantyr's daughter retrieves her father's sword from his ghost in the burial mound on Samsø.

The oldest source we have mentioning Berserkers is the Haraldskvæði, handed down in *Heimskringla* by Snorri Sturluson.

> They [the ships] were loaded with men and white shields, western spears and Frankish swords. Berserks bellowed; battle was underway for them; wolf-skins [berserks] howled and brandished iron spears.[103]

King Harald Fairhair also had Berserkers:

> But the king's twelve berserkers were in the part of the ship called the scissor. For the mentioned journey, Skallagrim chose the strongest and bravest men among his household and neighbours, twelve in number; many of them were hamrammr.[104]

When Grim, the son of Kveldulf, visited Harald Fairhair, after Harald had killed his brother, he brings along several that were 'Hamrammr' – shapeshifters:

> Kveldulf had in his hand a weapon of the kind called 'Brynjetrold' and then the berserk possession came upon him, as well as upon several of his people; they killed everything that got in their way.
>
> It is usually said that those who go berserk are so strong that nothing can resist them as long as they are in this state, but as soon as it has left them, they become much weaker than otherwise. That's also what happened to Kveldulf; when he had come to himself again, he felt so weakened by the fight that had just taken place that he had to go to bed.

Exhaustion, it seems, is the typical after effect of going berserk. The same story of exhaustion is told in the saga of Hervarar saga ok Heiðreks (authors unknown). The saga combines several stories:

> Hjalmar and Odd went up to the island to see if the Berserkers had arrived; but when they went out of the forest to their ships, the Berserkers descended from their ships, bloodied, and drawn swords. The berserker was then over; but then you become weaker than usual, just like after some kind of illness. Then Odd said:
>
> Once upon a time,
> that I feared,
> then the scrawny ones
> from the ships went,
> and with Howl
> the island climbs,
> empty of honour,
> twelve berserkers.

In the *Ynglinga Saga* it is stated.

> Odin could make his enemies blind or deaf or afraid in battle, but their weapons bit no more than sticks; but his own men went about without armor, and were mad as dogs or wolves, bit their shields, and were strong as bears or oxen; they killed people, but neither fire nor iron bit them. This is called berserk walking.

In the story of Kveldulf, from *Egil's Saga*, about the farmer who changed into a wolf in the evening, there is no mention of him leaving his clothes behind when he goes berserk, so this is clearly connected to 'Hamskifte' – shapeshifting. Kveldulf itself means evening wolf – he became a wolf in the evening, hence the name.

Loki is famously one of the gods who can shapeshift and he uses this ability on various occasions to get out of bad situations and save his hide when he has upset the balance. He could transform himself into various beings from human form to that of a horse and even a fly.

In the story about Idun, Loki borrows Freya's feather 'ham' in order for him to save her and bring her back to Asgaard. Then of course there is the story of how Loki shafeshifts into a mare and becomes the father of Sleipnir. In *Gylfaginning* we read about the origin of Sleipnir. Here an unnamed builder, a Jötunn, promises to build a fortress (Asgaard) for the gods in three seasons in exchange for the goddess Freya, the sun and the moon. The builder has a horse called Svaðilfari. With this horse the building of the walls progresses easily and three days before the deadline, the gods pressed Loki to find a way out of the deal. He turns himself into a mare and Svaðilfari becomes frantic and leaves work. After his dealings with Svaðilfari, Loki, as the mare, gives birth to the horse, Sleipnir.

> The wolf did Loki
> with Angrbotha win,
> And Sleipnir bore he
> to Svathilfari;
> The worst of marvels
> seemed the one
> That sprang from the brother
> of Byleist then.

This poem is preserved in the poem Hyndluljóð (the lay of Hundla), which is part of the *Poetic Edda.*

When Loki tricked the blind Hod into killing Balder with an arrow made of Mistletoe, he tried to escape the wrath of the gods by turning himself into a salmon. Just like Odin, he was very adept at shapeshifting, and there seems to be no limit to what shape he could take on. As Loki inhabits the border of what is socially acceptable, he sometimes shows an ambivalent relationship with shapeshifting; he often uses it as a form of self-preservation and the gods also rely on his abilities to get them out of a mess (which more often than not Loki has got them into).

Another example of shapeshifting that we have already touched upon is from the Nordic poem Bjarkemál, with the story of Bjarke fighting as a bear. While Bjarke sleeps in the hall, he shapeshifts and his doppelgänger in animal shape is fighting outside. When he wakes up, the bear has disappeared.

In the *Ynglinga Saga* we are told:

> Odin often changed his shape (Hamr); then the body lay as if asleep or dead, but he was then a bird or an animal, a fish or a worm, and went in an instant to distant lands, on his own or other men's errands.[105]

The animals were spirits aiding him to reach other worlds. To reach the world of the gods, animal spirits were also believed to have been mediators.

Anglo-Saxon illustrations and metalwork often depict zoomorphic interlace, a decorative style of art where animal shapes are entwined in a continuous loop. In Celtic and Norse tradition this is believed to symbolise a form of shapeshifting or perhaps shamanism, which the Anglo-Saxons believed in prior to Christianity.

An old Anglo-Saxon charm refers both to shapeshifting and 'Galdur' galdr, similar to the Norse concept.

> *One must take seven little wafers, as are used in (Christian) worship, and write these names on each wafer: Maximianus, Malchus, Johannes, Martimianus, Dionisius, Constantinus, Serafion. Then the charm that is mentioned hereafter must be sung, first into the left ear, then into the right ear, then over the crown of the man's head. And then let a virgin go to him and hang it on his neck. And do so for three days. Then he will be better.*
>
> *Here came striding in Upon/Within (a) spider-wight,*
>
> *He had his hama in hand, Said that you were his steed,*
>
> *Laid his fetter on your neck. They began to set off from the land;*
>
> *As soon as they had come away from the land, Then began his limbs to cool.*
>
> *Then came striding in The dwarf's sister;*
>
> *Then she ended it And swore oaths*
>
> *That this nevermore would be able To harm the sick,*
>
> *Nor him who this galdor Could acquire,*
>
> *Neither him who knew How to chant this galdor.*[106]

He has his hama in hand, could be his 'hamr'. There is no doubt the type of ailment or disease mentioned here is caused by an Otherworldly being who has targeted the patient with an Elf shot, a sudden and inexplicable pain of unknown origin. Before the conversion to Christianity, Pagan Anglo-Saxon society was rooted in the old Germanic traditions, The term *galdor* (plural *galdru*), meaning incantation, charm, or sorcery, derives from the Old English verb *galan*, 'to sing' or 'to chant'. It is rooted in Proto-Germanic 'gala' and is pretty much the same as the Norse 'galdr'. It was commonly used for magical chants in healing and protective contexts, as in the *Lacnunga* manuscript's Nine Herbs Charm, where the practitioner is instructed to 'sing this galdor' three times over herbs and the patient. As we can see the various terms such as 'Seidr', 'Galdr', and 'hamramr' (change of shape) were deeply inwoven in the art of healing and were very similar to earlier Norse traditions.

21

The Number Nine and Three

The number three, alongside number nine, is mentioned repeatedly throughout the sources. Three sons, three wives, have a fight against three knights. Ceremonies or incantations need to be repeated three or nine times. Whether they be stories with a magical purpose, fairytales or myth, or simply embedded in folklore, the numbers three and/or nine are needed for them to work.

Oral traditions usually have a certain rhythm with information that they present. They often contain parts of mythology mixed with actual events, sometimes making it hard to distinguish one from the other. This has often caused people to dismiss the events mentioned in these tales completely. We, however, would not be able to understand the world of the Germanic tribes, nor the folklore up through time, if we do not take these sources into account. Also, due to the importance of the stories to those that have been handing the tales down to us and those that have been told these tales, even if not entirely factual or true to events, they had a cause and meaning and resonated with people in a way they could explain the world.

It is clear with the number nine and three in Germanic myth, that the information we gain from the numbers shows the importance of them. In addition, the number three latterly became important in the Christian faith with the Holy Trinity. However, we can see the oral traditions have clear lines back in time, telling us it is not just a Christian tale.

Numbers nine and three are hugely prominent in the Norse world of mythology. We have the nine worlds of Yggdrasil and Odin hangs from the world tree, Yggdrasil, for nine days and nights in a self-sacrifice, to gain the knowledge of runes and to be able to see into other worlds.

The nine worlds are mentioned in *The Völuspa*:

I remember yet the giants of yore,
Who gave me bread in the days gone by;

> Nine worlds I knew the nine in the tree
> With mighty roots beneath the mold.[107]

And it is through *The Hávámál* that we read of Odin making his self-sacrifice by hanging in the tree of Yggdrasil for nine nights. In this verse it is Odin speaking of his accomplishment:

> Did I know I was hanging
> On a windy tree
> Nine whole nights,
> Wounded with Spear
> And given Odin
> Even myself,
> On that tree
> Like no one knows
> From what Root it originates.[108]

In *Vafthrudnersmaal* we are informed that Odin cast down Hel (goddess of the Underworld) into Niflheim, which lies under the roots of Yggdrasil, and gives her nine worlds that are to be the place for humans dying of old age and sickness.

> Of Giants and all
> Runes of the Gods
> I can tell the truth;
> For each a World
> Have I crossed
> To nine Worlds I came
> To Shadow Death down there –
> There wander the Dead from Hel.[109]

In Hermod's ride and the killing of Balder we hear that Hermod rides for nine long nights to get to Helheim to look for Balder.

> Towards this he rode for nine nights through deep and dark valleys, where he saw nothing, until he came to the river Gjöll and the bridge over it.

At Ragnarök, Thor is to battle the Midgard Serpent, dying from its venom after he kills it. In *The Völuspa* Thor takes nine paces and then drops dead from the venom. Once again, we have the number nine as a central part of the events. Thor here is of course the symbol of the ordered world, and the Midgard Serpent represents the forces of chaos, which is nature taking over. Nine is linked to the ordered world of the gods with Odin as its creator.

> In anger smites the warder of earth,
> Forth from their homes must all men flee;
> Nine paces fares the son of Fjorgyn,
> And, slain by the serpent, fearless he sinks.[110]

Draupnir, the ring of Odin smithed by skilled dwarves, drips every nine nights eight equal rings. So again, we have the number nine in connection with magical items and magic in general. Equally, Frey waits nine nights for his desired lover:

> We both know it –
> the profitable Lund.
> Maybe nine nights
> to Njörd's Son.[111]

In the lines below we are also told that the number nine is connected to sacrifices made by man.

> The young prince
> I owe my help,
> That after Relatives
> Paternal inheritance he reaches.
> An Altar he set for me,
> Built by Stene –
> Now they are Cliffs
> Turned into Glare –
> With the blood of nine oxen
> He sprinkled it.
> Always believed Ottar
> On Asynia. (Freya).[112]

In this poem Freya meets the Völva, Hundla. She is riding on her boar, Hildisvíni, and the Völva rides on a wolf. This shows again the close connection between animals and shamanism and the skills of Freya and the Völva as masters of seidr. The mission in the poem is to find the pedigree of Óttar. He worships Freya and builds her a Höerg (Hearg in old English). This is a sort of altar made of a heap of stones, built in nature as a place of worship. In this story he also offers a sacrifice to Freya with the blood of nine oxen. Again, the reference to the number nine is important in the beliefs.

In the same poem we hear of the number nine in connection with the Creation:

> One was born
> In the Morning of Time
> Greatly strengthened with Power,
> Of the Tribe of the Gods,
> The sword-adorned Hero
> Born of nine
> Giant (Jötunns) maidens
> At the Edge of the Earth.

Besides the Norse sagas, there are other sources that also mention number nine in connection with sacrifices. Thietmar of Merseburg wrote that people met every nine years at Lejre on Zealand in Denmark in January:

> and offer to their gods 99 people and just as many horses, dogs and hens or hawks, for these should serve them in the kingdom of the dead and atone for their evil deeds.[113]

Adam of Bremen gave a similar account in 1072 of the sacrificial traditions in Uppsala in Sweden:

> It is customary also to solemnize in Uppsala, at nine-year intervals, a general feast of all the provinces of Sweden.[114]

On the Stentoften rune stone that was erected in southern Blekinge in Sweden, we get confirmation of the meaning of the number nine and the sacrifices mentioned by both Thietmar and Adam of Bremen:

> Nine bucks, nine stallions, Haþuwulfar gave fruitful year, Hariwulfar ... I, master of the runes(?) conceal here runes of power. Incessantly plagued by maleficence, (doomed to) insidious death (is) he who this break.[115]

The male gender of the sacrificed animals might also have significance, along with the animal species chosen for the sacrifice. Hence the bucks could well signify Thor's goats, Tanngrisnir and Tanngnjóstr. Horses also have great importance in Norse myth and in this case it seems that Hariwulfar gains a good harvest by sacrificing nine of each animal he has chosen. The selection of the animals is not randomly chosen nor is the number of the beasts. The rune stone at Stentoften is believed to have been made around the seventh century and is a mixture of the old and new Futhark (the runic alphabets used by Germanic and Scandinavian peoples).

So, there is no doubt about the significance of the number of nine both when it comes to myth and that of the rites that took place amongst the Norse and Germanic peoples.

The number three also turns up in Norse myth but to a lesser degree than that of number nine.

Odin, for one, had two brothers making him one of three sons. In *The Völuspa* we hear of this:

> Then from the throng did three come forth,
> From the home of the gods the mighty and gracious.
> Two without fate on the land they found,
> Ask and Embla empty of might.[116]

Another mention of the number three in *The Völuspa* is the three Norns. The Norns are deities shaping the destiny of humans. In *The Völuspa* they pour water from their sacred well onto the roots of Yggdrasil, hence keeping the tree alive and vibrant. The well and water have a significant place in reaching the transcendent.

> Thence come the maidens mighty in wisdom,
> Three from the dwelling down 'neath the tree;
> Urth is one named, Verthandi the next, –
> On the wood they scored, – and skul the third.
> Laws they made there, and life allotted
> To the sons of men and set their fates.

Also. from *The Völuspa*:

> The war I remember, the first in the world,
> When the gods with spears had smitten Goolveig,

And in the hall of Hor had burned her,
Three times burned and three times born,
Oft and again yet ever she lives.[117]

The tree of Yggdrasil is supported by three roots. One root extends to the well of Urdr, which is perhaps called after the Norn of that name. Then we have the well of Mimir and finally the spring of Hvergelmir. So here again we have the number of three as part of the myth. These three roots are placed in different worlds in Yggdrasil. Thus, we can read in 'Grímnismál' in the *Elder Edda*:

Three Roots stretched out
Towards the edges
From the Ash, Yggdrasill,
Hel lives under one,
Frost Giants under the second,
True People under the Third.[118]

The significance of the number nine and three in the myths are echoed in folklore of later times. When doing some sort of ritual, it was usual to do something three or nine times for it to have any effect. An example from Orkney is the following cure mentioning nine knots.

> When a person has received a sprain, it is customary to apply to an individual practiced in casting the 'wresting thread'. This is a thread spun from black wool, on which are cast nine knots, and tied round a sprained leg or arm. During the time the operator is putting the thread round the affected limb, he says, but in such a tone a voice as not to be heard by the bystanders, nor even by the person operated upon…[119]

According to Danish folklore, if you want to take something from the elder bush where the elder mother lived, you had to ask three times while walking backwards. Only in this way was it safe to take something:

> Elder mother, elder mother, elder mother, please, may I take a bit of your forest.

Forgetting this could bring all sorts of bad luck to the farm's livestock or to yourself or people you knew. In Jens Kamp's *Dansk Folketro* (Danish Folk Beliefs), we learn:

> When you for the first time see the new year, you are to take a piece of bread and a coin in the hand and go outside the house. Look at the sun and say three times quietly. 'New year's let me never in this year have any less than I had the last.' Then you will have plenty in the new year.[120]

Another example is a rite from Bogø, an Island in Denmark. This is also from Jens Kamp:

> When a calf has been drinking some milk for the first time, the girl is to hit it lightly on the forehead and say, 'Drink yourself when I return', three times. Then the calf will be able to drink by itself in the future.[121]

There was also an old cure for warts, where you had to complete the ritual three times for it to work. In some places it is nine times, as there were regional variations. As we have just seen with the Anglo-Saxon charm against elf shots, it was to be repeated three days in a row for it to work.

These numbers are not random and are common in each enchantment. But as folklore is a mixture of old beliefs and new, there might in this be a little from both Pagan and Christian beliefs.

22

The Álfar/Fairies

As we shall see, the term 'fairy' potentially embraces a wide range of folkloric beings, many of which are briefly discussed below. As in all folklore, definitions are often vague at best, not least because they change over time and by region. This, of course, can make studying it all the more interesting.

The name álfar comes from Proto-Germanic 'albiz' (or 'alboz'), which in Norse became álfr, (álfar, plural), in Anglo-Saxon oaf and ælf (plural ylfe), and in modern English, elf. Álfr is thought to come from the root meaning of white and the álfar are described as brighter than the sun. Perhaps the álfr or ælf also comes from the proto Indo-European root albho, meaning white.

We should nevertheless distinguish between álfar and fairies, even though they are very similar. Fairies are of Celtic origin while the álfar are Germanic. There are no clear boundaries between them when it comes to British folklore. Some Celtic areas adopted stories of Germanic origin and vice versa. Simultaneously, the stories represent a mixture of cultures, meaning an intermingling of Celtic, Germanic, Roman and Christian (Roman) lore. In some cases when fairies are mentioned, it is really álfar we speak of. For example, Yorkshire folklore must have been influenced by Scandinavian myth, since York and its surroundings were part of what was called the Danelaw. The álfar have ties back to Proto-Germanic people, so the Saxons, Angles and Jutes would also have believed in these beings.

Álfr was in fact a popular component in Anglo-Saxon names, for instance male names such as Ælfræd, Alf-råd (modern form: Alfred). This gives clues that some Anglo-Saxons did believe in the álfar/elves. At the very least, it is highly likely that the beliefs would have been brought over to Britain by the Anglo Saxons and Jutes. The new arrivals, the Anglo-Saxons, kept their own beliefs; later they became Christians.

By the eighteenth century, fairies in folklore had become an overall concept for the various beings believed to exist, even though fairies were originally of Celtic origin and the álfar, Germanic. Thus, before the eighteenth century, fairies, like those mentioned in connection with Willy Howe, a round barrow in East Yorkshire, would most likely be elves.

By the time the Celtic and Germanic beings meet in British folklore, they are not identical but their characteristics and the stories about them are very similar.

For example, folklorist Thomas Wright identified the round barrow at Willy Howe which was said to be connected to fairies. The first reference we have to fairy folk in this place comes from William of Newburgh, a twelfth-century historian, himself of Anglo-Saxon descent, who states in his account that he had known about it since childhood.

Typically, in these stories, elves live similar lives to humans. They feast, dance and function just like humans, except that fairy lives take place in the old burial mounds, hills, forests or in other such places, away from the human realm. Also, they are believed to live longer than humans, in some cases immortality is even suggested.

In Norse mythology, the elf/álfr were discussed in tales around the god Frey and the álfar. Further, the *Younger Edda* of Sturluson contains several references to the álfar, where a distinction is made between the beautiful ljósálfar (light elf) and the svartálfar (dark elf or, dwarfs) i.e., between air and earth spirits. In the pre-Christian era, álfar were worshipped as gods, though not as prominently as the Aesir (the principal gods). In *The Völuspa*, álfar are mentioned as a distinct group, and some sources even point to them being the Vanir branch of gods.

> How fare the Aesir / how fare the álfar
> All Jotunheim groans / the gods are at council
> Loud roar the dwarfs / by the doors of stone,
> The master of rock / would you know yet more.[122]

So, the Aesir, the gods and the álfar seem to be closely associated and often mentioned together, although none of the álfar are ever specifically mentioned by name, only as a group. Some people have therefore suggested that the álfar are really the Vanir gods. As mentioned already, Frey was said to be the ruler of Álfheim (the realm of the elves). The home of the Vanir branch of the gods, Vanaheim, and Álfheim are both among the nine worlds of Yggdrasil that made up the Norse world view. We have no further description of Vanaheim, other than it being the home of the Vanir.

Even though no álfar are named specifically, there is no doubt that they held a prominent position and are often elevated to a higher status and associated with the Aesir (the Norse gods). This can be read in *Grímnismál*:

> The land is holy /that lies hard by
> The Aesir and the álfar together.
> And Thor shall ever / Thruthheim dwell,
> Till the gods to destruction go.[123]

And in *The Hávámál* yet again the Aesir and álfar are mentioned as two groups of gods:

> I can for the fourteenth time
> When I for the crowd of people
> The names of the gods must mention
> I know about everyone
> Aesir and the Álfar.
> The ignorant do not know such things.[124]

We then find this in the *Skírnismál:*

> Mær er mér tíðari
> en manna hveim
> ungum í árdaga;
> ása ok alfa
> þat vill engi maðr
> at vit samt séim.[125]
>
> To me dearer / than in days of old
> Was ever maiden to man
> But no one of the Aesir or the álfar will grant,
> That we both together should be.[126]

The Aesir and álfar are also seen in *Lokasenna*, another part of the sagas. The mention of the Aesir and álfar is seen fourteen times in the *Younger Edda* prose and, as seen below, several times in *Lokasenna*:

> Of their weapons they talk, | and their might in war,
> The sons of the glorious gods;

From the Aesir and Álfar | who are gathered here
No friend in words shalt thou find.

And again, later in the poem:

In horses and rings | thou shalt never be rich,
Bragi, but both shalt thou lack;
Of the Aesir and Álfar | here together met
Least brave in battle art thou,
(And shyest thou art of the shot.)

Be silent, Freyja! | for fully I know thee,
Sinless thou art not thyself;
Of the Aesir and elves | who are gathered here,
Each one as thy lover has lain.[127]

In this last prose Freya is accused of sleeping with all the Aesir and the álfar. If Freya needed to have sex with an anonymous group of supernatural beings, this suggests that in this account, the Vanir were in reality the álfar.

It has been suggested that the álfar were connected to an ancestral cult. This is very possible, given that the álfar are often associated with burial mounds in the landscape, and there was respect for the landscape of the dead. Fairies are indeed associated with burial mounds across Britain and in Scandinavia but if they are in fact connected to an actual ancestral cult lost to memory, the connection is not easily found in the sources. However, the respect people had for the burial mounds makes it very tenable. People avoided burial mounds, especially after dark, believing in the many stories of heavy punishment by Otherworldly beings if the peace of the mounds were disturbed.

The legend surrounding King Frode, who has been connected to Frey, points to some sort of ancestral or cult of the dead. In 'Þáttr Ólafs Geirstaða álfs' a story about Olaf Geirstade-Elf, a semi-legendary king of Geirstade in Norway, after his death, he is said to have been worshipped as an álfr. The story is preserved in *Flateyjarbók* (book of Flatey), a saga collection from the fourteenth century. The saga points to post-mortem worship of the king as an álfr ancestor, and details how the king instructed people to make his burial mound after he dreamed a prediction of a great famine striking the land.

It went exactly as Olaf had said and as he had interpreted the dream; sooner than had been expected, a great soot came, and many people

> died, and all the men were led to the hill, who seemed to have any access to it; for King Olaf let the men immediately depart from the Thing to throw up an exceedingly large mound, and the inhabitants of the country set about the enclosure which he had determined; it also happened that the herdsman died last, and finally King Olaf's burial took place, and he was hastily laid there with his men with much property, and the mound was then closed again; then the death of men began to abate; then followed a great storm and famine, and then the decision was made that they sacrificed to King Olaf for a good year, and called him Geirstadelf.[128]

Olaf's mother was Aløf from Álfheim, the realm of the álfar where Frey ruled. As we saw in connection with Odin and other gods, kings were often said to be descended from these deities. Here the bloodline goes to Frey and the álfar. They sacrificed to Frey 'år og fred' (meaning 'year and peace') as seen with the Álfablót.

The earliest mention of the álfar/elves in Britain is an Anglo-Saxon charm or spell against a sudden inexplicable pain believed to have been caused by elves shooting their invisible arrows (called elf-shots) at humans or livestock. It was generally understood that diseases were caused by sorcery – that the elves, along with witches and Otherworldly beings, could cause people to fall ill. However, their magic could be both malign and also benign. Elves and other beings, including witches, were blamed for various inflictions in cases of elf-shot.

James Henry Dixon, in his *Chronicles and Stories of the Craven Dales*, identifies two kinds of fairies in Elbolton, Yorkshire:

> The Craven fairies consist of two classes, the good and bad, or rather the mischievous. The former are those who on moonlight nights frequent green hills and pastures, and dance to sweet music breathed from reeds and oaten pipes. They are small, graceful creatures, and subject to a king and queen – democracy being unknown in the fairy world. They are fond of appropriate gifts but invariably resent improper or unseemly ones.[129]

We also have mention of the elf-shot in the William Collins (1721–1759), 'Ode on the Popular superstitions of the highlands of Scotland':

> By night they sip it round the cottage door,
> While airy minstrels warble jocund notes.

> There, every herd, by sad experience, knows
> How, wing'd with fate, their elf-shot arrows fly,
> When the sick ewe her summer food foregoes,
> Or, stretch'd on earth, the heart-smit heifers lie.
> Such airy beings awe the untutor'd swains.[130]

Here we are yet again told that elf-shot causes illness. Humans and livestock were usually struck by elf-shots because of some kind of considered offence to the Otherworldly beings. This is much like the narrative of the witch, who places a curse on a person who has seemingly wronged her in some way. A subsequent accident or sickness to humans or livestock proves the witch's curse must have been true.

Fairies are said to be fond of appropriate gifts, but also to make demands when it comes to respect. For this reason, people gave them small food and drink gifts to stay on good terms with them. Insulting a fairy could end very badly, a subsequent illness blamed on an elf-shot.

In places that people thought were connected to fairies and perhaps other mystical beings, the ground was dubbed either 'holy', perhaps deriving from the Anglo-Saxon 'Halige-Boden'(holy ground) as discussed in Dixon's *Chronicles and Stories*, or, according to some scholars, 'fairy ground'. Either way the ground was considered sacred by the local people and the beings thought to live there attracted both respect and fear, so much so that people gave them tokens and little sacrifices to keep on good terms with them.

As discussed in earlier chapters, animism means that nature is animated. The fairy mounds are offshoots of that belief. The ground is not sacred in the same way as a churchyard, but the place might have been a sacred ground in the pre-Christian era. Burial mounds and hills were believed to be haunted by fairies and other spiritual beings and were highly respected; many were likely only preserved because of the beliefs in resident elves/fairies.

In his account, Collins notes that he saw numerous beings, especially people – both men and women – but he does not mention any size variation. It was not until much later that the elves or fairies were described as smaller than ordinary humans. Thus, the considered appearance of fairies and their various forms have changed over time. During the period Collins was writing, they were the size of normal humans. As with Scandinavian cases, they simply had magical properties, and many of them were considered god-like and were honoured as gods before the Christian era.

There are stories in which humans marry fairies and have children. Usually, they end badly; Elias Owen calls them taboo stories.

> All the current tales of men marrying fairy ladies belong to a class of stories called, technically, Taboo stories. In these tales the lady marries her lover conditionally, and when this condition is broken, she deserts husband and children and hies back to fairy land.[131]

All these stories from Britain, Scandinavia and Germany are similar, pointing to some sort of root back in time, at least back to when the Anglo-Saxons came to Britain and settled. From then beliefs and folklore surely mingled, perhaps receiving a revival with the Vikings. In some cases, we certainly find the lines in folklore going back even further.

23

The Fairy/Elves Cup

The tale of the fairy cup is a typical narrative in folklore. In most of these stories the cup ends up in human hands as they flee the pursuing fairies. In Thomas Wright's description, we are also told that in fairy lore, a human approaching a fairy mound or living place and seeing them partying, will immediately be offered a drink. However, if they drink this beverage, they will be carried off to fairy land.

> One day a rustic of the village just mentioned, went to visit one of his friends in a neighbouring village, (no doubt North Burton) the road to which lay near our tumulus, a road, therefore, which we may easily suppose people would not then willingly choose to pass at night. However, the love of beer, which was then even more powerful than at the present day, kept the rustic visitor until a late hour at night, and when at length he started on his way home he was at least all the happier for his entertainment. As he approached the tumulus his astonishment was great to hear merry sounds issued from it, which betokened that it was occupied by a party who were feasting and singing. Wondering who could have come to that lonely spot to enjoy themselves at such an hour, he approached nearer to the mound, and then, for the first time, he saw a door open in its side. Our rustic friend, who was well mounted, rode boldly up to this door, looked through it, and beheld, inside, a spacious apartment, brilliantly illuminated, and a large company of men and women seated at a magnificent entertainment. As he stood there staring at the door, one of the cupbearers, seeing him, approached and offered him the cup to drink. Now it must be remarked that, according to the doctrines of fairy lore, (for these were fairies,) when a mere mortal approached

> their assemblies accidentally, the fairy-folk always offered him some of the liquor they were drinking, and, if he drank it, he immediately lost all power of returning home, and was carried away into fairy-land. But the rustic of East Yorkshire was too wise for that, for he poured the contents on the ground, and, grasping firmly the cup, started off at full gallop. The fairy feasters rushed from the tumulus and gave chase; but the horse of the fugitive was a good and swift one, and almost by miracle he reached his village in safety and secured his valuable prize. He had, however, a chance in his favour which William of Newburgh had forgotten to state. It was an article of popular belief, equally in the time of the fairies and in that of the witches, that if you once placed a running stream between yourself and your unearthly pursuers, they had no longer any power over you. At a very little distance from Willey-hou the stream of the Gypsies must have protected the fugitive in his flight to Wold-Newton. His prize turned out to be a vase of unknown material, and equally strange in form and colour, (vasculum materiae incognitae, coloris insoliti, et formae inusitatae). This extraordinary cup was soon talked of far and near, and at last it was given to King Henry I – for it was in his reign that this event occurred. Henry subsequently presented it to his brother-in-law, king David of Scotland; and many years afterwards the second king Henry, visiting the Scottish court, was shown this wonderful cup, and begged it of William the Lion, who then occupied the Scottish throne. 'This story', says William of Newburgh, 'may appear strange, and people would not believe it if it had not been attested by the most trustworthy witnesses'.[132]

According to this tale, if a human drunk from the offered cup, the human would be carried off into fairy land, likely never to return home. For any that were lucky to return home, they would discover that the time passed in fairy land appears shorter than in the human world.

The Danish stories are strikingly similar but with a slight twist. In these, the late-night wanderer sees the mound, which is stood on four burning poles, the feast taking place inside the mound. As soon as he approaches a beautiful elven woman, a troll, mountain man or similar greets him with a drink. But in the Danish case, he tosses the drink over his shoulder and rides off with the cup. Some of the liquid lands on the horse's back, burning its hair, strongly suggesting that the drink is dangerous for the man. In the Danish cup stories, there is usually no mention of the victim being sent to fairy land. This happens in other tales but, otherwise, the stories are similar almost to the letter.

This account is from Evald Tang Kristensen, a Danish folklorist and schoolteacher, who was born in 1843 near Kolding, Jutland in Denmark.

> Bondededde, a witty and more enlightened man than the common crowd, and who knew more than other farmers, lived in Tornved farm, where the previously mentioned burial mound is right next to it. He was the son of a mermaid and therefore knew everything that the Otherworldly beings and the trolls did to them, which he successfully prevented. Therefore, they persecuted him a lot. One Christmas Eve, one of them called out to him. He, who understood it immediately, goes out into the yard, sits on his sharp-shod stallion, which was safe. When he rides outside the farm, someone hands him the mentioned goblet or vessel, from which he was to drink. But he threw this drink behind him, when some drops that fell on the horse's back immediately took off the hair. He then rode at full speed to the church, followed by the trolls, threw himself from his horse over the fence, and was now safe there until morning, when he set out for home again. He then presented the cup to the Church. Peter's Church, 1808. Herman Boss.[133]

The narrative of the golden goblet becoming the altar cup of the church is repeated all over Denmark. The similarities between the Danish stories and the English one from Willy Howe and other such places in Britain is striking and cannot be random. The account of the man being taken to fairy land likely comes from a post-eighteenth-century mixture of Celtic and Germanic myth.

As we have seen, the description of the beings has also changed over time, folklore often absorbs various traditions and is impervious to fixed boundaries. Folklore is truly a mixture of various beliefs which shift through the centuries.

Another element of the myth surrounding Willy Howe also has connections to the pre-Christian era:

> There is a certain air of quaintness about the rhymes which seems to speak for the antiquity of this legend. The peasantry assures you further that if anyone runs nine times round the tumulus without stopping, and then puts his ear against it, he will distinctly hear the fairies dancing and singing in the interior. The old superstitious

> feeling relating to the spot seems, indeed, to exist almost as strong amongst the peasantry of the present day as it did ages ago; our proceedings excited general alarm among the lower classes, who expected to see some manifestation of vengeance on the part of the beings believed to hold the guard of the tumulus; and few would have ventured out in its neighborhood after dark.[134]

We have already seen that the number nine is significant, in Germanic, and Norse mythology. This area of Yorkshire was populated by Danes in the Viking age, as well as being connected to the Anglo-Saxons. So, even if stories involving elves and fairies had not survived the Anglo-Saxon conversion to Christianity, they were rejuvenated with the Danish incomers in the Viking age. Guthrum, who came with the Great Heathen Army, ruled his kingdom from York after the peace treaty with Alfred the Great. Later the area became associated with the Danelaw. Of course, the stories changed over time, adding and removing layers but we can see in the lines back to the pre-Christian era along with hints of Norse and Anglo-Saxon beliefs before their conversion to Christianity.

24

The Fairy Rings

A fairy ring is a turf circle found on lawns or in grassy areas, often delineated by the growth of mushrooms. In folklore it was believed that the ring was made by fairies dancing in a circle.

> He and the other children of the hamlet used constantly to amuse themselves by running round and round in these rings; but they had always been religiously careful never to run quite nine times round any one of them. 'Why not?' I asked. 'Why, sir, you see that if we had run the full number nine times, that would have given the fairies power over us, and they would have come and taken us away for good, to go and live where they lived'.[135]

The children were afraid to go around the circle nine times, as it was believed that the fairies would gain power over them if they did. As demonstrated over and over again in folklore, nine and three were necessary for magic to work.

Normally a fairy ring consists of a natural growth of fungus but on the Shetland Island of Fetlar, we find a stone circle named Haltadans. It was said that the stone circle was actually petrified trolls who had been dancing, and that the two stone pillars in the middle was the fiddler and his wife. In England, on Dartmoor in Devon, a rock surrounded by a ring is called the Pixies' Church.

In England it was common belief that stepping into a fairy ring would cause bad luck or even turn people insane. At the same time, it was believed that it was the entrance to the Otherworld. Even Shakespeare mentioned these rings, advising people to tip toe around the ring so as not to disturb the fair folk:

> If you see a fairy ring
> In a field of grass,
> Very lightly step around,

Tiptoe as you pass;
Last night fairies frolicked there,
And they're sleeping somewhere near.

Usually, the belief was that if you entered the fairy ring you might be forced to dance until you drop or be carried off to the Otherworld as punishment for intruding on the 'Good Folk'.

In Denmark this natural phenomenon was called a 'Heksering' – witch ring, despite the fact that the folklore surrounding them were closely linked to the álfar. It was believed you could get sick if entering the ring. In Germany this phenomenon is known as 'Hexenring' and was believed to be places where the witches danced on Walpurgis night, a night where the veil between worlds was believed to be thinner and any herbs gathered that night would be more potent; the meaning and consequence of entering such a ring was the same as that in the British cases. A fairy ring can be considered as a liminal space where one could enter into the Otherworld, just like burial mounds and crossroads.

25

Burial Mounds and Natural Hills as Fairy Ground

A fascinating detail about the Willy Howe round barrow is the fact that the barrow has attracted many legends and much lore and yet several excavations have been conducted but no burial remains have surfaced from either the Anglo-Saxon or Viking periods. However, some pre-Christian rituals might have taken place there, resulting in its reputation as being a place of álfar/fairy activity.

In some cases, even natural hills get associated with burials and álfar/fairies. In the *Norse Sorceress* you can read about this in connection with Gunnar's burial site in *Njál's Saga*, the longest saga from Iceland. This is a natural hill that was turned into a burial mound in the stories, and was visited and painted by the British painter William G. Collingwood. It seems any pre-Christian rituals there had been forgotten, as the site became known as a fairy place.

> Collingwood's painting makes clear that the mound that he was shown was not a real funeral monument, but a natural hill only local folktales turned into a place of burial. After a millennium, the historical ritual had faded from memory, and its props had shifted to new locations.[136]

Another place worth mentioning in this connection is an old oak forest near Stevns on the island of Zealand in Denmark. This forest was believed to be the Elven King's soldiers, the trees awakening after dark. Local peasants refused to enter the forest during nighttime hours for fear of these elves. It is possible that rituals from the pre-Christian era took place here, thus, turning it into an elven place. Indeed, perhaps Frey, the ruler of Álfheim, was worshipped in this very forest; consequently later generations of people believed elves lived there.

> Near Store Heddinge Church you can find traces of an oak forest. Once upon a time, there were elven king's soldiers who had the form of trees during the day, but at night they were fearsome giants.[137]

Memories of such a grove or sacred ground as this could linger for a very long time, even though people no longer really remember the reason why the place was considered sacred. This can be seen in all of the above cases.

You might think that these traditions would not have survived the transition to Christianity and that the memory of the old ways would have vanished as the centuries passed, but this was not the case. The description of these Otherworldly beings and the way they were worshipped continued long into Christian times, leaving no doubt that these beings originated from the pre-Christian Era with roots far back in time.

As we have seen, groves, trees and water areas were all used as places to reach the transcendent in the pre-Christian era. These places became liminal spaces where transition could take place. This explains why elves were believed to live in these mounds, hills, forests, and waterways, because they were portals between the human world and the Otherworld, as outlined in Norse myth. Similarly, on days such as Samhain or Walpurgis Day, when it was thought that the veil between the worlds was thinner, it was believed that ordinary people could have contact with these Otherworldly beings.

There are many stories connected with these mysterious mounds, and mostly they reveal that digs on such sites are rarely successful. Those digging for treasure must do it in absolute silence. If a word is spoken, the treasure sinks into the ground, never to be seen again. Willy Howe is connected to such a story. Yet again we must return to the writings of Thomas Wright.

> This is not the only legend which the peasantry of the neighborhood has preserved relative to Willey-hou. They tell you gravely that years ago some avaricious personage dug into the tumulus in order to gain possession of the treasure it was supposed to contain. At length, after much labour, they came to an immense iron chest, the receptacle of the coveted riches, but the lid was no sooner uncovered than it lifted itself up a little, and out sprang an immense black cat, which seated itself upon the chest, and glowered with eyes of fire upon the insolent intruders. Not daunted by this, after making various ineffectual attempts to move the chest, the digger for treasure fixed to it a strong chain or rope, to which he attached

> so numerous a team of horses, according to some accounts, or bullocks, according to others, that they reached two and two from the tumulus to North Burton, a distance of full a mile and a half. When all these preparations were completed, the director of these operations gave the order for moving exultingly in the following words – of course addressing his animals:
>
> 'Hep Joan ! prow Mark!
> Whether God will or no,
> We'll have this ark.'
>
> He had hardly uttered the words when the rope and the traces broke in a hundred places, and the chest of treasure disappeared forever.[138]

In this story from Thomas Wright, the perpetrator digs and finds the chest but loses it again. This frustrating quest was a common theme – the moral of this and other similar tales seems to be not to touch the burial mounds. In some of the Danish versions of the tale, the consequences see either a farm or the whole village going up in flames. When people rush to the place to extinguish the fire, they find everything is in order. This pattern can repeat itself numerous times until people stop digging.

In Denmark there are similar stories about the mounds containing treasures and, as with Dixon's story, the diggers lose the treasure the moment they utter a word.

> On a hill near Markskjælbæk, (Denmark) between Fol and Harreby, some men were once digging for treasure. While they were working, they saw Harreby on fire. They paid no attention to it but continued digging. Then a cart came driving by, drawn by four mice. The people were also completely silent at that. After that, someone came riding on a stump-tailed cock and asked: 'Haven't you seen Grönjung coming by?' When no one answered, he said: 'Yes, just let her go, I'll catch her soon enough'. Then one of the people could not remain silent any longer and said: 'You can catch the devil!' With this the treasure sank ten cubits deeper since such digging must be done silently.[139]

In this case the Otherworldly being, a dwarf or álfr, provokes the diggers to speak. The notion is the same as above. To get the treasure, one must remain completely silent, otherwise, the treasure will be gone for good.

Though the light álfar seem to be those living in Álfheim, we need to be aware of the dark álfar/elves (Dökkálfar) too, not least because of the stories of treasure. The dwarves, who were also known as the dark elves, were associated with treasure due to their excellent work as smiths. The dark álfar are thought to be dwarves, but in folklore the stories often mix dwarves and (dark) álfar, perhaps suggesting that these beings' roots are mixed. It is unclear what the distinction is between the dark elves and the light elves and the origin of the dark elves is highly debated. What we can say is that the Disney version are a very much modernised variant of what was portrayed in the Brother's Grimm fairytales and their predecessors.

Size is something which differentiates the Scandinavian álfar or elves. The light elves, the very elves dancing in the mist, are often normal human size. They are usually described as beautiful women, luring men to get involved in their dance. With the dwarves/dark elves in burial mounds, their horses are the size of dogs etc. In Denmark, it was believed that tiny elves were living under the oven in a house, under the floor or alternatively in burial mounds. Many of these are sometimes considered as a 'Nisse', a sort of brownie (discussed further in the next chapter). They are helpful, benevolent creatures, if their understanding with humans is upheld, which means giving them little sacrifices of food to keep them happy. In many cases they were offered a sort of sweet porridge with butter and beer for their farm work. They were sometimes called mountain folk, despite them not living in the mountains.

> In a place in Skørping, (Denmark) there were mountain folk under the people's oven. The mountain folk were going to have a wedding, and the human woman living there lent them things they needed for the wedding. Therefore, she was allowed to see the bridal party, but she received a slap because of it. It came straight through the room and had a lame fiddler; he struck out with his leg and smashed the dish of wine to pieces. The woman laughed at that, because she could see it, and her husband slapped her, because he could not see anything. The wedding lasted three days, and then they carried the things back again.[140]

The word troll is 'Trold' in Danish, which relates to the Danish word 'trylle', meaning magic. That is what trolls are: beings with magical properties. When the Danes mention trolls, they can be referring to various kinds of magical beings, such as elves, mountain folk, Nisse, goblins or nixies/Nøkk. They were all able to do magic; they could be very large or very tiny, to huge and ugly or very beautiful. Therefore, the word troll in myth is different to how we understand it today, as a rather dumb and anti-social giant. It just meant a being able to do magic and beings said to live in the mounds in Denmark are variously described as trolls, dwarves, or mountain folk.

26

Hobgoblins, Goblins, Brownies, and the Scandinavian 'Nisse' or 'Tomte'

Aside from fairies and elves, there are a whole host of other mystical beings to be found in folklore and myths. Many of these are considered household spirits, and feature heavily in British folklore, with roots stretching back to Denmark and Scandinavia. All have similar traits or characteristics but differ by name and geographical location. The brownie or broonie heralds from Scotland and we find tales of the hobgoblin in England. These beings are similar to the Danish/Norwegian Nisse and Swedish Tomte or the German Kobold. They all date to the pre-Christian era, although belief in them remained even after Christianity took hold in the later centuries.

We begin with goblins and hobgoblins, which are similar terms but represent quite different beings. Goblins have a European origin and are small, grotesque-looking beings, who are mischievous at best, but very often ill-tempered and malignant. A hobgoblin is more of a household sprite, that was more mischievous than anything else. In some cases a hobgoblin, similar to the brownie, Puck, or the Danish 'Nisse', if teased or offended, could turn into a Boggart – a nasty malign creature much like a poltergeist and known for its pranks. A Boggart was a malign spirit which could wreak havoc, and the only way to rid oneself of such a fiend was to get the help of one or more priests.

Another word for the álfr (Norse for elf) is Ellyll, which can mean an elf, demon, or goblin. A description from Elias Owen tells us:

> The third name given to the fairies is 'Ellyll', an elf, a demon, a goblin. This name conveys these to the land of the spirits, and makes them resemble the oriental Genii, and Shakespeare's

> sportive elves. It agrees, likewise, with the modern popular creed respecting goblins and their doings.[141]

According to *Brewer's Dictionary of Phrase and Fable* from 1898, Robin Goodfellow was the name given to the Hobgoblin. Hob was a thirteenth/fourteenth century nickname given to someone named Robert or Robin, which became associated with Robin Goodfellow and thus household goblins became hobgoblins. This is an example of the good-tempered hobgoblins who can also pull pranks and be mischievous.

> Robin Goodfellow is a 'drudging fiend', and merry domestic fairy, famous for mischievous pranks and practical jokes. At night-time he will sometimes do little services for the family over which he presides. The Scots call this domestic spirit a brownie; the Germans, Kobold, or Knecht Ruprecht. Scandinavians called him the Nisse god-dreng. Puck, the jester of Fairy-court, is the same.[142]

'Nisse' derives from the common Danish name 'Niels' and 'god-dreng' meaning good boy.

A hobgoblin is believed to be a household spirit or creature from central and northern England. It could live inside a farm or household or somewhere outside. In Yorkshire's Runswick Bay, some caves are named the 'Hophole' in view of the perceived connection with hobs. The Reverend George Young explains in *History of Whitby and Streoneshalh Abbey*:

> Curious caverns are sometimes formed in the alum-rock by the operation of the tides. Hop-holes in Runswick Bay once presented a most romantic appearance, the entrance being divided by a double pillar, as in the annexed drawing. This cave is still 70 feet long, and 20 feet wide at the entrance; but the pillar is now gone. Another aerial being, which we may supposed to have been a hobgoblin, had his dwelling in the Hop-hole, near Runswick. He was more benevolent than Jeanie; for his powers were exercised in curing young children of the hooping-cough. When any child in Runswick or the vicinity was under that disease, one of its parents carried it into the cave, and with loud voice thus invoked the demi-god of the place; 'Hob-hole Hob! My bairn's got kink-cough; take't off!' it is not very many years since this idolatrous practice was dropt.[143]

Here the hobgoblin not only helps bring prosperity to the farm but also cures children of diseases. The hobgoblin here was believed to be a cave resident rather than being connected to a specific farm. However, he seems to be a protector of the land and serves as help to the local human population in a geographically confined area.

It was also believed that at night, the hobgoblin would arrange for impossible chores to be done:

> This was but one of the many exploits of a like nature achieved by this well-willed being in aid of the work on that favored farm. In the barn, if there was a 'weight of work' craving to be done, and time was scant or force insufficient, Hob would come unasked, unwarned, to the rescue, and the corn would be threshed, dressed, and sacked, nobody knew how, except that it was done by the Hob.[144]

Unnatural strength was attributed to the hob, and he was often credited with completing the chores that the humans had struggled to accomplish.

Hobgoblins and álfar, and the way they were worshipped, have roots back to the old household gods or demigods. These hobgoblins also share similarities with dwarves, who are described as living in rocks and caves. We are told here that hobgoblins might also live in caves. Like all traditional folklore, the stories contain a mixture of various beings and context. We have seen that elves could also live in places of nature, in burial mounds and under the stoves in houses. Wherever they live, the importance of these beings to the prosperity of the household remains very significant and is as meaningful as it was in the pre-Christian era. The little tokens these beings were given show a link to the sacrifices that were once made to the old household gods or Otherworldly beings who were considered protectors of the land.

The festival of 'Álfablót', as discussed earlier, gives us some idea of how these beings were worshipped in the pre-Christian era, although the sources do not tell us in detail how the worship was performed. As Sigvat Tordsson, the author of the poem 'Austrfaravísur' discovered, he was not allowed to enter a house where a family were celebrating Álfablót' as the festival was a private affair to the family, and the householder feared the wrath of Odin if she allowed him in. In later descriptions, we are told that the beings are given food and drinks to perform their helpful tasks. Since we know that people sacrificed animals such as pigs, sheep, and/or cattle to the gods before the Christian era, it is not far off to imagine that this may also have been part of the Álfablót. In the same way as people continued such rituals when worshipping these beings in the Christian era.

Once you had a hobgoblin or a 'Nisse', attached to your household, it seems it was often impossible to get rid of it. A Dane compares the hob and 'Nisse', in this regard:

> 'In England', says Worsaae, 'one may hear many a tale told, just as in Danish lands, about the tricksiness of the Nisse (Nix). On one occasion during my stay in England, it occurred to me to tell our northern story about a "bonde" (a word nearly equivalent to our English "yeoman") who was teased and annoyed in all sorts of ways by a Nisse. At last, he could not stand it any longer, and he determined to quit his holding, and to go to some other spot. When he had conveyed nearly all his movables to his new farm, and was just driving the last load of all, he happened to turn round, and what was the sight that met his eyes? Nothing less than Master Nisse himself, red cap, and all, calmly perched on the top of the load. The small chap nodded with provoking familiarity, and added the words, "Ay, here we are, flitting"'. But there is no play on the vowel in Worsaae's Danish. It is just the ordinary Danish phrase, 'Nu flytte vi', [now we move] which is employed.[145]

You cannot outrun the pranks of a hobgoblin who has decided to harass you, so you might as well take what comes or try to appease the 'Nisse' or goblin. According to Reverend Atkinson, Worsaae found this Danish tale repeated almost word for word in Lancashire. A large part of what was Lancashire was also part of what was previously Northumbria, which was conquered by the Danes in AD 866–867, the region becoming part of the Danelaw. This likely explains the similarity of the stories from both Britain and Denmark.

Hobgoblins and 'Nisse' are usually described as solitary, short, often hairy men, very similar to the description of a dwarf in northern mythology. The Nisse in Scandinavia is described as a pipe-smoking little man. Dobby is another word for hobgoblins in Lancashire and Yorkshire. Again, it is possible that they have a common origin but it's equally possible that a mixture of myths is involved. The Irish myths, for example, were written down before the Norse invasion, so we can say for sure that the Tuatha Dé Danann and the Sídh folk or Aos Sí originate from the Celtic myths. Writing in the seventh century, the Irish Bishop Tirechán described the Sídh folk as 'earthly gods'.

In Scottish folklore, the brownie was originally described in the oldest stories as normal human size, and hairy like the hobgoblin, but as with the fairies, they seem to have shrunk over time to become short in stature. According to folklore, the brownie can shapeshift into animal form. This is also the case with the 'Nisse' and 'Tomte', who could often change shape into a horse. Being invisible is also common but this is an ability it seems most fairies have. There is a marked similarity with the Roman Lares, a household god in the Roman religion who protected the home and community.

> Brownies were reputed to attach themselves to families, doing the work of a man-servant or a maid-servant. They were short of stature, had wrinkled faces and curly brown hair and wore a brown mantle and hood. Some haunted ruins of old castles or dwelt in hollow trees. They lived to a great age. One was reputed to have dwelt in Leithin Hall in Dumfriesshire for three centuries, and when he deserted it the owner of the hall met with ruin. A male Gruagach is referred to in some parts of the highlands and resembles a brownie. He usually wears a beaver hat and carries a wand. Many tricks are played by him. Like the female Gruagach, he receives offerings of milk, which is poured into a hollowed stone called Clach na gruagaich, or over a slab called leac Gruagaich.[146]

Here, the brownie was closely connected to a specific building, but they could also be attached to a specific place in the landscape. This is the same with the 'Nisse' and 'Tomte' of Scandinavia. Though brownies seem a more peaceful race, both the hobgoblin and brownie could easily be offended. However, the hobgoblin is more prone to playing practical jokes; giving them clothes could cause them to leave.

> Blue Burches is the name of a shapeshifting hobgoblin who played harmless pranks in the home of a shoemaker and his family on the Blackdown Hills in Somerset. His usual form was that of an old man wearing baggy blue breeches, but he also took the form of a white horse, a black pig, and a wisp of blue smoke.[147]

This so-called Blue Burches haunted a family in Somerset with his pranks. It is fascinating to see the animals he can shapeshift into. The horse is yet again present, and it is a white horse – as we have seen in the Celtic world, Oisin rides on a white horse and the colour white is strongly associated with the Otherworld. The 'Nisse' could also turn himself into a horse as well as other animals. Blue Burches could also change into a pig; in Denmark, the 'Nisse' could turn himself into a ram.

The Anglo-Saxons brought their Pagan beliefs with them when they came to Britain and the horse, pig, and ram were all important animals. The animals that appear in these tales are not random – the old beliefs lived on in some form up through the centuries.

In Denmark, the 'Nisse' is said to be similar to the 'elle' folk, the elves, and the trolls but more benign towards the human population.

> The Nisse was of the same kind as the Mountain folk and Elle folk, but more distinguished and also the farmer's benefactor and idol, whom they worshipped on Lørdag/Saturday, like Frej on Friday and Thor on Thursday. (Vedel Simonsen)[148]

The Scandinavian word for Saturday is 'Lørdag' coming from the Norse root 'Laugardagr', which literally means 'washing day'. Perhaps the Nisse or ancestors or those little gods connected to the family and farmstead were worshipped on this day. At least this is the case according to Vedel Simonsen (1780–1858), a Danish historian. Much like many of his time, he showed great interest in the beliefs and folklore of ordinary people.

That these 'Nisse' were worshipped, suggest that some rituals must have survived, in a changed form, and continued to be part of the daily life of the ordinary people even up to the modern day. Of course, such rituals would have contained some parts of the Christian faith, but Simonsen is very specific that people worshipped these little house gods on specific days.

Often payment for the help of a brownie, hobgoblin or 'Nisse' was a little food and milk or beer.

> Offering of meal and milk are supposed to appease the fairies. All milk spilled upon the ground is supposed to reach either them or the small subterranean demons known as the Fridean.[149]

In Denmark, the food was mostly a kind of sweet Porridge with butter on top and beer. For Christmas today there is even a beer called 'Nisseøl' – Nisse beer – a light beer only sold at Christmas time. The Nisse demanded his payment either once a year, at Christmas, or sometimes once a week depending on the local tradition, but to deny him his payment could make him very angry.

The Scottish brownies also have much in common with the dwarves and elves of Scandinavia. According to Elias Owen, there were at least two kinds of fairies in Scotland – the brownies, and the fairies. The brownies were so called because of their tawny colour and the fairies because of their fairness. The Brownies look different to the fairies, but both are fairies, just as we saw with light álfar and dark álfar. They fall under the same umbrella term but differ in looks and nature.

Fairies are most often described as beautiful women whereas brownies were little men, in much the same way as we see dwarves. We can even see this in the story of *Snow White*, published by the Brothers Grimm in 1812 ('*Sneewittchen*' being the original German title). The seven dwarves who work in the mines bear a huge similarity to the folkloric beings we have in British and Scandinavian folklore, once again showing a link to the Germans or Germanic tribes that stretched back in time to the Anglo-Saxons.

One story from Deiri, Yorkshire, appears to almost have been taken directly out of the Danish realm. Yorkshire was, of course, the centre of Danelaw and therefore heavily influenced by Danish settlers, law, and rule. In a chapter of his *Historia rerum Anglicarum* (History of English Affairs), William of Newburgh relates as follows:

> In the province of the Deiri (Yorkshire), not far from my birth-place, a wonderful thing occurred, which I have known from my boyhood. There is a town a few miles distant from the Eastern Sea, near which are those celebrated waters commonly called Gipse.... A peasant of this town went once to see a friend who lived in the next town, and it was late at night when he was coming back, not very sober; when lo! from the adjoining barrow, which I have often seen, and which is not much over a quarter of a mile from the town, he heard the voices of people singing, and, as it were, joyfully feasting. He wondered who they could be that were breaking in that place, by their merriment, the silence of the dead night, and he wished to examine into the matter more closely. Seeing a door open in the side of the barrow, he

went up to it and looked in; and there he beheld a large and luminous house, full of people, women as well as men, who were reclining as at a solemn banquet. One of the attendants, seeing him standing at the door, offered him a cup. He took it, but would not drink; and poured out the contents, kept the vessel. A great tumult arose at the banquet on account of his taking away the cup, and all the guests pursued him; but he escaped by the fleetness of the beast he rode, and got into the town with his booty.

The scene of this legend, we may observe, is the very country in which the Danes settled; and it is exactly the same as some of the legends current at the present day among the Danish peasantries. It is really extraordinary to observe the manner in which popular traditions and superstitions will thus exist for centuries.[150] When we compare the Danish stories with the British, they can be strikingly similar down to the smallest detail. The only part which is not mentioned in this story from Yorkshire is the consequence of the drink poured on the horse. In the Danish stories, the horse's hair and flesh are burned off by the cup's content. Here is another such story:

A man from Lellinge had gone to cook for his master. When he was riding home late in the evening, he passed a troll (fairy) hill, and he could see that it was completely lit up. As he rode by, a small gray creature came out and handed him a cup of wine to drink. He also accepted the cup, but poured the wine down over the horse's back, and then he hurried away at a strong trot. The troll pursued him to get his cup back and was just about to catch up with him. Then the man came past another troll hill, and there stood a troll in the opening, who was an enemy of the first troll who pursued the man. That troll then shouted to him:

'Ride away from the lumpy one and out onto the bolder one'. (This means the plough furrows. It was believed the trolls had difficulties crossing the furrows the plough had made.)

He did so, and now the troll could not follow him. He then managed to get home safely. But when he came to the farm, the horse fell, and it now appeared that where the wine

> had been poured on it, the flesh had been eaten right down to the bones. The cup was very valuable and remained on the farm.[151]

This is one example among many where stories heralding from Yorkshire are notably like those from the Scandinavian area. This also applies with the German stories and fairytales found in the Brothers Grimm.

27
Changelings

A constant fairy and álfr motif were the changeling – a human child kidnapped by fairies and swapped with a fairy child. According to the stories, this often happened when a human child was left unattended. The changeling features in Irish, Scottish, Welsh, English, Scandinavian, and German folklore. Usually, the fairy child left in the human world had either a disability or was disfigured in some way – features such as a big head, or other visible abnormal traits. The stories were one way of explaining congenital disabilities, however in these cases, people fully believed that their child had been taken and a fairy child left in its place. Both elves and fairies were believed to be prone to taking a human child, and stories from the Celtic and Norse areas are very similar when it comes to changelings. Elias Owen writes about this belief:

> It was firmly believed, at one time, in Wales, that the Fairies exchanged their own weakly or deformed offspring for the strong children of mortals. The child supposed to have been left by the Fairies in the cradle, or elsewhere, was commonly called a changeling.[152]

This narrative was also common in Scandinavia and in Germany. This is from the Brothers Grimm:

> During the first six weeks following childbirth, mothers may not go to sleep until someone has come to watch the child. If mothers are overcome by sleep, changelings are often laid in the cradle. To prevent this one should lay a pair of men's pants over the cradle.[153]

The idea that mother and child are at risk from the time of childbirth until the child can be presented in church comes from the notion that people are specifically vulnerable during transition phases, such as the passage from childless woman to mother, or spinster to marriage, in other words where a status change is involved. The idea is the same as the belief that on specific dates you need to be more careful than on others, to make sure the Otherworldly beings or witches do not take people away.

> In Fiskgård in Sir, many years ago, there lived a man called Ole Murer. In his time, there were Mountain folk (Fairies) under the garden belonging to the farm, and often on bright summer evenings the little ones were seen frolicking among the bushes. Then it happened that Ole's wife gave birth to a child, and the mountain folk took it and then put another tiny creature in its place. It was a real pity to see him when he got older – he never grew big, and he never became wise either. Some said quite rightly that he was no changeling, but that a mountain man was his father, and that Ole's wife his mother. It is true that as long as he was on the farm, there was prosperity in Fiskgård, but when he left, the wealth dwindled.[154]

A typical characteristic of a changeling is that the child never grows to normal size and displays unusual behaviour. A similar story is told about a child from Islay at Gart na Damh – as long as the child was alive, the family and farm prospered. When the child died, the family's luck dwindled.

In the legends of Scotland, Wales, and Ireland, we are told how to reveal that a changeling was a fairy child. In a story from the West Highlands, a young boy falls ill and takes to his bed. His father is confused, desperate to regain his son's health. An old man comes to his door and reveals how he can find out if his son had been taken away by fairies and replaced him with one of their own:

> 'I will tell you how', answered the old man. 'But, first, to make sure that it is not your own son you have got, take as many empty eggshells as you can get, go with them into the room, spread them out carefully before his sight, then proceed to draw water with them, carrying them two and two in your hands as if they were a great weight, and arrange when full, with every sort of earnestness, round the fire'. The smith accordingly gathered as many broken eggshells as he could get, went into the room, and proceeded to carry out all his instructions. He had not been long at work before there arose from the bed a shout of laughter, and

> the voice of the seeming sick boy exclaimed, 'I am now 800 years of age, and I have never seen the like of that before'.[155]

In these stories the child often turns out not to be a child but a fairy with a long-life span.

The use of eggshells is also seen in the Danish stories, though sausages made from a young pig were more common. This story was collected by Evald Tang Kristensen, a Danish folklorist:

> A wise woman gave her the advice that she should take as many eggshells as she could get her hands on and throw them under the pit kettle when she was brewing beer. She should then place the child in front of the fire, so that it could see the many eggshells in the fire. Then she should go out into the utility room and lie in wait to hear if the child would speak. When she had placed the child and hidden herself, it began to say: 'Now, I have lived so long that I have seen Rold forest planted and cut down thirty times, but I have never seen anyone brew beer with eggshells'. The woman now jumped in and shouted: 'Then you are not my own child, but a hideous old troll, whom I have now dragged along for three whole years'. Then she seized a stove rake and began to beat the troll. It helped, because now her own child came falling down the chimney, but with a broken arm, and the ugly troll disappeared immediately.[156]

In the Danish stories, the elven or troll woman usually turns up when the fairy changeling is threatened with fire or is being beaten, saying 'I have treated your child better than you have mine'. Or in the case of the story with the old child or fairy, he vanishes up through the chimney.

Yet again the Brothers Grimm have collected stories involving eggshells similar to tales we see in Scandinavia and Britain:

> A mother had her child taken from the cradle by elves. In its place they laid a changeling with a thick head and staring eyes who would do nothing but eat and drink. In distress she went to a neighbor and asked for advice. The neighbor told her to carry the changeling into the kitchen, set it on the hearth, make a fire, and boil water in two eggshells. That should make the changeling laugh, and if he laughs it will be all over with him. The woman

did everything just as her neighbor said. When she placed the eggshells filled with water over the fire, the blockhead said:

> Now I am as old
> As the Wester Wood,
> But have never seen anyone cooking in shells!
> And he began laughing about it. When he laughed, a band of little elves suddenly appeared. They brought the rightful child, set it on the hearth, and took the changeling away.[157]

The way to regain your own child was often rather brutal. Sometimes it was suggested to leave the child outside to be exposed to the elements. The parents were advised not to go out to the child until it had stopped crying. The implications of this are harrowing, considering the child may have been disabled or sickly, but of course we must remember that people strongly believed that their child was a changeling. In this story from the West Highlands, we are told of another way to get rid of a changeling. This story comes from the folklore collection, *Popular Tales of the West Highlands*, by J. F. Campbell:

> You must light a very large and bright fire before the bed on which this stranger is lying. He will ask you, 'What is the use of such a fire as that?' Answer him at once, 'You will see that presently!' and then seize him and throw him into the middle of it. If it is your own son you have got, he will call out to save him; but if not, this thing will fly through the roof.[158]

The father was then told by the old man to venture to the mound of the fairies where they kept his son on a certain night bringing a dirk, a bible, and a cockerel. That he was to bring a cockerel has a connection to an old Norse myth. Gullinkambi (meaning golden comb) is a rooster living in Valhöll/Valhalla. In *The Völuspa*, Gullinkambi is one of the three roosters whose crowing will signal the beginning of Ragnarök. Along with other items, roosters or hens were believed to have magical properties. The importance of the cockerel is also pointed out in the book, the *Norse Sorceress*:

> Special roles of cocks and chickens are also clearly emphasized in non-Norse texts that pertain to the ritual activities of Scandinavian societies. In *Gesta Danorum* for instance, the Danish chronicler Saxo Grammaticus mentions a woman who throws a cock's head over an unusual barrier and into the Otherworld. In the

> Otherworld the bird miraculously comes back to life, regardless of its incompleteness of its body.[159]

In the account of the Arab chronicler, Ibn Fadlan, on the Rus Viking burial, a cockerel and a hen were initially sacrificed, among other animals. This points to a belief of birds, chicken or cockerels being able to reach the transcendent, thus in this case perhaps the cockerel was necessary to gain entrance into or connect with the Otherworld to retrieve his child that had been stolen by the fairies.

According to Elias Owen, writing in the nineteenth century, the cockerel was associated with the devil, so over time the cockerel has been demonised by the Church. He goes on to inform us:

> The Romans also used birds for divination. In the legend of Remus and Romulus, Remus saw some birds first, but Romulus saw a greater number. It ended with Remus being killed and Romulus building the City of Rome. One of the well-known methods of divination in Rome was to consult the sacred chicken – these chickens were considered oracles, another illustration of the importance of birds when it came to communicating with the Otherworld.

The use of Hazel was yet another way to have your child returned:

> One mode of bringing back the true child was the following. A new skull [an oblong basket] was taken and hung over the fire from a branch of a hazel tree, and into this basket the suspected changeling was laid. The careful watch was kept till it screamed. If it screamed it was a changeling, and it was held fast to prevent its escape. When an opportunity occurred, it was carried to a place where four roads met, and a dead body was carried over it. The true child was restored.[160]

Hazel was considered a source of wisdom and could protect against malign magic as previously discussed. Thus, Hazel would also reveal a changeling. This way of revealing a changeling is strikingly similar to the water trials of witches. Individuals (usually women) suspected of being a witch would be subject to trial by water. If the accused person floated, she was a witch; if she drowned, she was not a witch. Yet again this was a particularly harrowing way of disposing of a child believed to be a changeling.

The crossroads represented a liminal space between the worlds and was also considered a way to reach the fairy world or the world of various Otherworldly beings. This would be similar to the man entering the fairy hill equipped with the Bible, a cockerel, and a dirk. In *De falsis diis* written by Ælfric of Eynsham, we are told that Mercury, who is here representing Odin, is worshipped at a crossroads:

> There once lived a man named Mercury, who was very deceitful, and, though quite wise in speech, was treacherous in actions and lies. The pagans, in their account, also made him their great god and often and frequently offered him sacrifices at crossroads, through the teachings of the devil, and to high hills they often brought various offerings of praise.[161]

This means that both the Anglo-Saxons and Vikings worshipped Odin at these liminal spaces before their conversion to Christianity. Later, witches were said to meet at crossroads to conjure the devil. It is not surprising that crossroads later became associated with the devil since the old Pagan ways often became demonised.

It was also believed that fairies were particularly active in taking children on St John's Eve, 23 June, a date that today merges Christian traditions (as the feast of St John the Baptist) with ancient summer solstice rituals.

> It was believed that the Fairies were particularly busy in exchanging children on Nos Wyl Ifan, or St. John's Eve.[162]

This was due to the belief that the veil between worlds was thinner on this day, much as we have seen at Samhain. St John's Eve along with Walpurgis night (the night before 1 May) was believed easier for Otherworldly beings to interact with the human population. The same is sometimes true in some Danish tales.

In some cases, older children or adults were taken by fairies. One common belief warned against interacting or dancing with fairies, lest people got carried off into the fairy world. People especially vulnerable could be in a transitional phase of their lives, such as just before getting married or giving birth to a child etc. In Welsh and Scottish stories, many victims seem to be men drawn in by sweet music and wanting to dance with the fairies to their beautiful tunes. Thus, the victim would become spellbound, entering into the fairy world and remaining there unheard of in the human world, sometimes for many years.

Often the marriage of a fairy female or a human female was involuntary as described in this Danish story. The woman is dragged off at night, bewitched by the magic of the troll or elves, and made to marry. The green boys are male elves and 'Elle' is the Danish folk name for elves.

> The Elle folk or the green boys were so nasty. They took all kinds of things and carried them away, including people. A midwife out near Egelykke had a daughter who was soon to be married. But she came to look so pale and ill. So, they kept watching over her and then saw that two green boys came in through the window and took the girl with them while she was sleeping. She resisted a bit, but they got her out and dragged her into a mountain (mound). The mother followed and saw that they were putting her at a mill, and she was supposed to grind on it. They had not got the door closed after them, and so she hurriedly made a cross and threw herself in there. Then everything fell together, beams and everything, and there were a scream and a wail. The midwife had pulled her daughter out in the same moment. The latter then said that one of the days she was supposed to have a wedding with one of the green boys, but she had not been able to tell that before. Teacher Engberg's wife, Havborup. Langeland.[163]

The girl was unable to talk about the green boys before she was rescued, due to the magic they had put on her.

A couple of stories from Funen, the island in the middle of Denmark, tell of brides being taken into the fairy realm after fairies came to dance with them. They think themselves only gone for a few hours, but in reality, years have passed. This fits with the notion or belief that you are particularly vulnerable to the fairies or elves when in a transitional part of your life.

> THE OLD BRIDE
>
> Once upon a time there was a Wedding in Munkebo. The bride went outside the farm during the dance and without thinking about it came to a hill in the field, where there was dancing and merriment among the 'Elle people'. When she got all the way to the hill, she saw that it stood on red poles, and a man came to her and offered her a cup of wine. She drank the wine and was invited to dance. But when the dance was over, she went back to the farm. Then she thought that everything had changed; she knew neither the farm nor the houses and no one had heard anything about the

> wedding feast, and when she entered the farm, there was no one she knew, and no one knew her. An old woman, whom the bride cried out to, exclaimed: 'So it is you who disappeared a hundred years ago at my grandfather's brother's wedding'. At these words, the old bride fell over and died on the spot.[164]

A similar story is told from Nørre Broby, also a small town on Funen. The bride is drawn to the music of the 'Ellefolk' and she does not return until many years later, and she subsequently dies immediately after, out of sheer fright when finding out that so many years has passed. In the tale from the town of Broby, we are told that the bride is trapped in the fairy mound after being lured in by the music and the merry dancing.

28

Means by Which You Could Avoid Malignant Sorcery

Given the belief in Otherworldly beings, it was only natural that people developed ways and rituals to protect themselves from any perceived danger. Elias Owen tells us about some of the means with which the stealing of a child could be prevented:

> There were, however, effectual means for protecting children from their machinations. The mother's presence, the tongs placed cross-ways on the cradle, the early baptism of the child, were all preventives. In the Western Isles of Scotland fire carried round a woman before she was churched, and round the child until he was christened, daily, night and morning, preserved both from the evil designs of the Fairies.[165]

As with Danish folklore, baptism was believed to be the most effective means with which to protect the child. However, the cross would also do the trick. Fire, as they used in the western isles of Scotland, is also an effective means to protect folk from harmful magic. As seen on Samhain and Walpurgis night, bonfires were lit to protect people from Otherworldly beings, evil spirits etc. Fire was believed to have a cleansing and purifying effect. This was also the reason why people accused of witchcraft were punished with fire – it was to purify and clean their souls of sin.

Iron or steel placed in the cradle was also an effective means by which you could protect your child from being taken by fairies. Fairies appear to be allergic to iron or steel. Similar phenomena are seen in German stories. According to the Brothers Grimm, a key or some part of the father's clothing was to be placed in the child's crib. The key would be of iron, so here we see the same idea in Britain, Scandinavia, and Germany.

Other means of protection could be petrified sea urchins, petrified octopus and stone axes used against various kinds of malign magic. Folklore from

Denmark and southern England shows that petrified sea urchins (meaning a sea urchin fossil) and stone axes were called 'thunderstones', thought to have been thrown to earth by Thor. The word thunderstone is believed to be a loan word from old Norse stemming from the Viking Age. The petrified sea urchin was believed to have magical properties from the megalithic period and has been used as an amulet since then, right up to modern times. A grave dated to the early Bronze Age in Bedfordshire, known as the Dunstable Echinoid burial and containing a mother and child, also contained a large number of petrified sea urchins, showing a most impressive number of these fossils. This detail tells us that the urchins had some magical or religious meaning to the people involved with the burial.

> Most curious of all was a large number of fossil Echini from the chalk. At first twelve were detected surrounding the girl, but at last, on extending the grave, nearly 100 were found. On repeatedly shovelling and raking over the earth from the entire tumulus, 200 or more were found, and most of these, undoubtedly, originally belonged to the girl's grave, as none were found in the other graves. Two species were represented, one the 'fairy-loaf,' Ananchytes ovatus, Leske.[166]

In Denmark on the island of Funen, a very special grave, the Blidegn grave, was found dating to around AD 100. The woman buried here is believed to have been a sorceress, and her grave contained numerous seemingly odd objects, among those several twigs wrapped in some wool thread, part of a stone axe and a sea urchin. Another deviant grave containing a man, found at Trekroner, near Roskilde in Denmark, likewise contained a petrified sea urchin. Normally males are not found with grave content, which often suggests sorcery. However, this male was different, in that it was also found that he had a severely underdeveloped arm. We do not know whether he was born with this defect or if the arm had withered away during his lifetime. Perhaps this deformity made it possible for him to reach the transcendent in some way.

> Another grave that stood out was A2066, which contained several antiquities scattered in the fill and at the bottom of the grave. It was a fairly large fill of 251 x 208 cm, in which a man was buried. Among other things, three knives and two weights were found near the skeleton. What was remarkable was the filling process, where burnt bones were added together with shards of pottery.

> High in the fill was found, among other things, glass beads, a small bowl-shaped fibula without a needle and a quarter-penny weight, as well as several short iron nails, a coffin hinge and two petrified sea urchins. The majority of the antiquities were thus not found near the skeleton but distributed in the upper 50 cm of the grave's fill. Furthermore, it is striking that while the skeleton is anthropologically assessed to be that of a man, several of the antiquities are of types traditionally associated with women.[167]

The content of these graves shows clearly that sea urchins and stone axes had a long tradition as protective amulets, very possibly being used in various rituals in pre-Christian times.

In Denmark, the petrified sea urchin was known under various names including 'Smørlykke' (Jutland) and 'butter luck' (meaning it brought luck to the making of butter). On Funen we have the words 'Smørsten' (butter stone), and in Odsherred, 'Smørdrue' and 'Smørhøne' (butter grape and butter hen respectively). In eighteenth-century Denmark, sea urchins were referred to as 'spådejesten' (similar to the word for fortune teller – 'Spåkone') perhaps linking the wise women and perhaps the Völva in the pre-Christian era to the sea urchin. They were believed to have magical properties which the wise women could use in their magical work.

In part of Western Scotland these squid fossils, called Bat stones, were to be put into water to cure distemper, as people believed they had healing properties. In southern England, grinding them into a powder was thought to heal rheumatism and sore eyes.

In Scandinavia, petrified squid were believed to be the light of the Vættr/Otherworldly beings, so named because people thought it was with those that the Vættr lit their homes, hence the name 'Vættelys' vættr – gnome's light. In all cases, these fossils were believed to have healing properties, as well as acting as a protective shield against harmful magic. In Scandinavia, they were considered a protection against lightning, and were often placed under the roof as lightning-shields.

In Dorset, petrified squid were called Col Pixie fingers, fairies being called Col Pixies which could take the shape of a small pale horse or pony.

29

Will-o'-the-Wisp, Ellylldan

Will-o'-the-Wisp are ghostly lights seen at night especially in swamps, bogs, and marshes. These beings led people astray by shining their light, leading people to think it was a lantern. According to Wirt Sikes, Ellylldan was a species of elves in Welsh folklore that correspond to the English Will-o'-the-Wisp. In Scandinavia we have the 'Lyktgubhe' in Swedish, and in Danish 'Lygtemænd' (translated as 'light men').

> The Ellylldan is a species of elf exactly corresponding to the English Will-o'-wisp, the Scandinavian Lyktgubhe, and the Breton Sand Yan y Tad.[168]

This common feature in the folklore of Britain was also seen across Europe and given various different names. According to the folklore, these beings were apparitions of men who had committed some despicable deed. According to the lore, these souls were doomed to wander the land for all eternity, perhaps because they had moved poles marking the fields, thus, stealing land from other farmers, or for any other misdemeanour; in their wanderings they haunt the living, their spirits never at rest. Some believed they were the restless souls of unbaptised children.

> The dialect terms denoting the ignis fatuus, or Will-o'-the-wisp, are some masculine and some feminine names; or again, they may denote an unpersonified apparition – e.g., corp-candle, corpse-candle (Sc. Lan. Lin.); dead[death]-candle (Sc.) – regarded as an omen of death. Among these names are: Billy-wi'-t'wisp (w.Yks.); Hobbledy's-lantern (War. Wor. Glo.); Hob-lantern, Hobby-lantern (Wor. Hrt. e.An. Hmp. Wil. w.Cy.); Jack-a-lantern (in gen. dial. use), cp. 'Jack with a Lantern,' Johnson, Dict.;

> Jenny-burnt-tail (Nhp. Oxf.); Jenny-wi'-t'-lantren (Nhb. n.Yks.); Joan-in-the-wad, or Joan-the-wad [bundle of straw] (Som. Cor.); Kit-in-the-candlestick (Hmp.); Kitty-candlestick (Wil.); Kitty-wi'-the-wisp (Nhb.); the Lantern-man (e.An.); Peg-a-lantern (Lan.); Peggy-lantern (Lin.); Pinket (Wor.). This lantern-bearing sprite haunts bogs and swampy meadows, where it gambols and dances by itself.[169]

The ghost lights haunted bogs and swampy areas according to the lore recorded by Elizabeth Mary Wright. As illustrated above, these Will-o'-the-Wisps went by many different names according to geographical location, but behind the different names we find the same characteristics. They supposedly lure people to their deaths by shining a light out in the bog or on the moor. Will-o'-the-Wisps make people lose their way on known paths, and they would find themselves getting lost and walking in circles in places they had never got lost before. One way people could get out of this predicament was to turn their clothes inside out, as this supposedly broke the magic. As with most fairies, they were neither entirely benevolent nor malign. In Danish folklore you could ask the 'Lygtemand' to show you the way, giving him a silver coin.

> It was at the close of just one of these tedious, wearisome expeditions that the farm-servant on one of the farms in Fryup Head was losing out his weary 'draught' (team), and the willing farm-lass was lending a helping hand, when they saw in the swampy, undrained 'swang' lying some quarter or third of a mile below the house on the border of the beck, a will-o'-the wisp, or in local nomenclature, a 'Jenny-wi'-t'-lant'ren'. The man turned his jacket inside out and the girl turned hers.[170]

The idea of carving scary faces in Turnips is not limited to one singular place. Turnips were also carved with scary faces and a light was placed inside to scare of evil spirits in Denmark, as was the case in other places in Europe. As we have seen, the Vikings celebrated similarly around Samhain, and it is possible that the tradition derives from this. In the eighteenth century Halloween, as we now know it, was called All Saints night, and it was a common tradition in all of Europe. Turnips were used in Europe, but when immigrants brought the tradition with them to America, they started carving a pumpkin instead. This then returned to Europe where we today still carve pumpkins at the end of October.

30

Selkie, Seal Folk and the Mermaids, Water Spirits

From Britain, we find a host of stories of mortal men taking fairy women as their wives.

Selkies

A Selkie is a shapeshifting being in folklore who has seal skin – the word Selkie is of Scottish origin, meaning seal, but the shape of these beings can vary. For example, the Selkies in Lanarkshire, Scotland, are like big horses. They are also called Selkie folk. There are various spellings such as silkies, sylkies, or selchies.

In the stories about the Selkie women, they can no longer live in the ocean after a human man has taken their seal skin – they are left following them to shore, pleading to them return their skin. The men refuse and in the end the Selkie woman agrees to marry the man and live with him for several years.

Here is an extract from one story told on Orkney.

> Well, it happened one day that the goodman of Wastness was down on the ebb (that portion of the shore left dry at the low water), when he saw at a little distance a number of selkie folk on a flat rock. Some were lying sunning themselves, while others jumped and played about in great glee. They were all naked and had skins as white as his own. The rock on which they sported had deep water on its seaward side, and on its shore side a shallow pool. The goodman of Wastness crept unseen till he got to the edge of the shallow pool; he then rose and dashed though the pool to the rock on its other side. The alarmed selkie folk seized

their seal skins, and, in mad haste, jumped into the sea. Quick as they were, the goodman was also quick, and he seized one of the skins belonging to an unfortunate damsel, who in terror of flight neglected to clutch it as she sprang into the water. The selkie folk swam out a little distance, then turning, set up their heads and gazed at the goodman. He noticed that one of them had not the appearance of the seals like the rest. Then he took the captured skin under his arm, and made it home, but before he got out of the ebb, he heard a most doleful sound of weeping and lamentation behind him. It was that one of the selkie folk whose seal skin he had taken. She was a pitiful sight; sobbing in bitter grief, holding out both hands in eager supplication, while the big tears followed each other down her fair face and ever and anon she cried out, 'o bonnie man! If there's onie mercy I' thee human breast, gae back me skin! I cinno' cinno' live I' the sea without it. I canno' canno' cinno' bide among me ain folk without my ain seal skin. Oh, pity a peur distressed, forlorn lass, gin doo wad ever hope for mercy theesel'. The goodman was not too softhearted, yet he could not help pitying her in her doleful plight. And with his pity came softer passion of love. His heart that never loved women before was conquered by the sea-nymph's beauty. So, after a good deal of higgling and plenty of lovemaking, he wrung from the sea-lass a reluctant consent to live with him as his wife. She chooses this as the least of two evils. Without the skin she could not live in the sea, and he absolutely refused to give up the skin. So, the sea-lass went with the goodman and stayed with him for many days, being a thrifty, frugal, and kindly goodwife. She bore her goodman seven children, four boys and three lasses, and there were no bonnier lasses or statelier boys in all of the isle. And though the goodwife of Wastness appeared happy, and was sometimes merry, yet there seemed at times to be a weight on her heart; and many a long longing look did she fix on the sea. She taught her bairns many a strange song, that nobody on earth ever heard before albeit she was a thing of the sea, yet the goodman led a happy life with her.

Now it changed, one fine day, that the goodman of Wasteness and his three eldest sons were off in his boat to the fishing. Then the goodwife sent three of the other children to the ebb to gather limpits and wilks. The youngest lass had to stay at home, for she

> had a beelan foot. The goodwife then began, under the pretence of house-cleaning, a determined search for her long-lost skin. She searched up, she searched down; she searched but, and searched ben; she searched out, and she searched in, but never could she find, while the sun wore to the west. The youngest lass sat in a stool with her sore foot on a cringlo. She says to her mother, 'mam what aredoo leukan for?' 'O bairn, deu no tell,' said her mother, 'but I'm leuking for a bonnie skin, tae maka Rivlin that wad ceur thee sare fit,' says the lass, 'May be I ken whar hid is. Ae day, when ye war a' oot, an' ded tought I war sleepan I' the bed, he teuk a bonnie skin doon; he gloured at it fir a perrie minute, folded hid and led hid up under dae aisins abeun dae bed.' (Under the aisins – space left by slope of roof over wall-head when not beam-filled.) When her mother heard this, she rushed to the place and pulled out her long-concealed skin. 'farewell, peerie buddo!' (a term of endearment), said she to the child, and ran out. She rushed to the shore, flung on her skin, and plunged into the sea with a wild cry of joy. A male of the selkie folk there met and greeted her with every joy token of delight. The goodman was rowing home and saw them both from his boat. His lost wife uncovered her face, and thus, she cried to him: 'goodman o' Wasteness, fareweel tae thee' I liked dee weel, doo war geud tae me; bit I lo'e better me man o' the sea!' and that was the last he ever saw or heard of his bonnie wife. Often did he wander on the sea-shore, hoping to meet his lost love, but never more saw her fair face.[171]

Selkies or selkie folk are found in traditions in many places of Europe but prominently in the Celtic and Germanic world. They are similar to the seal folk found on the Faroe Islands.

The Kópakonan: The Seal Folk of the Faroe Islands

On the Faroe Islands in the north-east Atlantic (between Scotland and Iceland) it was believed that the seal folk were voluntary suicides in the ocean. On the thirteenth night of the year, they could go ashore and shed their skin, and look like any other human, in that form to dance and play the whole night on the rocky beach or inside the seal caves.

Legend has it that a young man from Mikladal, on the north Faroe Island of Kalsoy, had heard that the seals used to gather at a cave near the village on certain night of the year, so he went there that evening to see whether or not it was true.

Near the cave was a rock which the youngster hid behind. After sunset he saw many seals swimming ashore and taking off their seal skin, laying them on the beach, whereupon they really did look like ordinary people.

The young man thought it fun to stay behind the rock watching the seal people. While there, suddenly he saw an unusually beautiful girl slip out of her seal's skin and fell in love with her immediately. He noted where she put her skin, crept over, grabbed it, and then hid again behind his rock.

As with the story from Orkney, the seal girl eventually finds her skin again, but only after having lived with the young man for years. After she escapes, the human husband goes with the rest of the people from the village on a seal hunt. She warns him in a dream not to kill specific seals because they are her seal husband and sons. He does not listen to the warning, and she returns with a curse, stating that the men of Kalsoy will either die at sea or suffer cliff-falls, until there are so many dead that they could reach all around the island holding hands.

The story's core is the same as the one from Orkney. The mortal human steals her seal skin, and he loses his seal woman when she finds it again. In the story from Orkney, the seal woman also has a seal man, just like the seal woman from the Faroe islands.

In this example, the story appears to be closely linked to the Norse part of the world. The story from the Faroe Islands contains a seal woman's curse, although the selkies normally do not harm humans. That characteristic usually belongs to the mermaids/men and other water spirits, not the selkies. The stories involving selkies are found mainly in Scotland and the western parts of Ireland but to a lesser degree also occur elsewhere in Britain, but here in the Faroe Islands' tales of the selkies are merged with other types of merfolk or water spirits.

Tales similar to those of the Faroe Islands and the Orkneys are also found in stories from Iceland. Here, Jon Arnason wrote a collection of Icelandic fairytales which also mention 'Selshamurinn' (The Seal-Skin).

The earliest mention of selkies is found in a medieval text and many more similar stories come from the Norse sagas. The stories of the Selkies, the sirens, the mermaids and the mermen are often intermingled and are seen across the world in various shapes and sizes in folklore.

In the collection of Scottish tales, *Wonder Tales from Scottish Myth and Legend*, we are told of the wonderous city at the bottom of the sea where the king of the seals live. In this story the seal hunter is unwittingly taken to this very city by a stranger, who later is revealed to be the son of the king of the seals. The seal hunter is to heal the seal. In the quote below the seal hunter sees the light at the bottom of the sea and discovers he, himself, has changed shape into a seal:

> At length he saw a faint green light, and as he went onward the light grew brighter and brighter, until the glens and bens and forests of the sea kingdom arose before his eyes. Then he discovered that he was swimming beside the stranger and that they had both been changed into seals.[172]

In this story we are told that they live similar lives to those of humans. Women are nursing their young and seals are going forth and back, living their lives at the bottom of the sea.

We read a similar tale in *Folklore of the Isle of Man*, published by A.W. Moore in 1891, where it is stated that:

> a splendid city with many towers and gilded minarets, once stood near Langness, on a spot now covered with sea. Here merfolk dwelt, surrounded by treasures they'd accumulated they had caused to sink.[173]

In Wales, it is suggested that the seal folk are human beings who have returned to the sea as merfolk. This points to the similar story from the Faroe Islands who believe that Selkies are people who have committed suicide by throwing themselves into the sea or people lost at sea for other reasons. However, in Wales it is a wilful transformation, and doesn't need to involve suicide.

Sea-fairies or seal folk can turn a seal-hunter into a seal, although we are not told how this happens. The hunter is unwittingly given a sealskin to wear when entering the water. We are told that the seal folk cannot live in the water, unless they have the correct skin, and they take it off when walking on land.

> The fisherman was startled to realize that the old seal on the bed was the very one he had tried to kill, and his heart was filled with fear. He threw himself down and begged for forgiveness and mercy, for he feared that he would be put to death.
>
> The guide lifted up the knife and asked: 'Have you ever seen this knife before?' He spoke in human language. 'That is my knife, alas!' exclaimed the fisherman.

> Said the guide: 'The wounded seal is my father. Our doctors are unable to cure him. They can do naught without your help. That is why I visited your house and urged you to come with me. I ask your pardon for deceiving you, O man! but as I love my father greatly, I had to do as I have done.'[174]

In this tale, the man had stabbed the old seal with a knife made of iron or steel; iron or steel was a known way to break fairy-magic. This explains why only the seal-hunter could help and heal the old seal. The seal-hunter is told to lay his hand on the wound, and the old seal is instantly healed.

After the old seal has been healed, the seal-hunter is made to promise he will never hunt seals again. In return, the seals promise him good luck with fishing in the future so he will prosper. Then, he is brought back to the surface to live his life there.

In this same story we also hear of the seal's love for music, a fondness which they have in common with other fairies. The seals promise they will help him catch fish but in return ask him to bring along a fiddler to play music for them as a reward when they do so. This tells us that they are as fond of music as all fairies we learn about in folklore.

Some people claim to be descended from these various mermaids, selkies, sea-fairies or water-spirits, one such example being the Scottish clan, MacCodrum. In Gaelic, 'Clann Mhic Codruim nan rón' means Clan MacCodrum of the seals.

Mermaids and Mermen

The selkies have distinct properties which distinguish them from mermaids, who are usually depicted as half-human, half-fish. In the stories these two different kinds of beings are not always kept apart but are mixed with each other. However, their characteristics differ. The selkies are usually said to be seen in groups, including when they appear on the coast as humans.

The mermaid, however, is more often seen alone on a cliff combing her long golden hair. Here, she carries a mirror and a comb, and her song is seductive, like that of the siren from Greek mythology. The English word 'mermaid' derives from 'mere' (sea) and maid. Mermaids or water creatures/spirits are mentioned across the world, including Europe. Folklore stories have various kinds of merfolk, intermingled through time, reflecting the mixing of the various cultures, whilst also giving the tales a local twist. The mermaid is also connected to the sirens as depicted on Greek vases from the ancient times. The most famous mention of these sirens and their seductive song is in the epic poem, *The Odyssey*, in which Odysseus and his crew are warned by the sorceress Circe about their irresistible song. Odysseus is tied to the mast and his crew stuff wax into their ears, to avoid the song of the mermaid. The mermaids were often believed to be the cause of shipwrecks and the death of sailors.

We find the mermaid/man or water-fairies in the Faroe Islands, Scandinavia, The Isle of Man, Ireland, England and all the way to the Classical world of Greece and Rome. In Britain, mermaids are often portrayed as evil omens who foretell storms.

The *Physiologus* (or bestiary), originally written in Greece probably around the third or fourth century, was a manuscript that gained much attention in the medieval era. Thus, the narrative of the half-human, half-fish became a common theme in folklore.

Another medieval text that had a profound effect on the concept of the siren was the *Liber Monstrorum*, a bestiary describing various creatures. It was written in the seventh or eighth century in Anglo-Saxon England, describing the mermaid as half-human, half-fish.

In the Norse world we have the god Njord as a god of the ocean. He lives in Nóatún, which means shipyard, and is connected to shipping and fishing. The ocean itself was connected to the Jötnar, and the giants Ægir and Rán. They had nine daughters who personify the waves – each name of these daughters is another name for a wave (again we have an instance of the number nine).

The name of the Jötunn, Ægir, means ocean in old Norse. Rán is said to catch sailors in her fishing net, then drag them down into the ocean to drown. Ægir is well-liked by the Æsir gods who visit him. We hear of this in the saga of Ægir's banquet.

Jötnar are not to be considered evil, they simply represent the forces and consequences of nature. In this case, they bring along violent storms, that cause shipwrecks and resultant loss of life, ships, and cargo. Rán is mentioned in various places such as the *Prose Edda*, as well as in the *Völsunga Saga*, and *Friðþjófs saga hins frœkna*, as well as in 'Sonatorrek', a skaldic poem, which appears in *Egil's Saga* written around 1220–1240. The poem speaks of the death of the poet's two sons, one dying of fever and the other drowning in a storm. In the *Völsunga Saga,* Rán lends her net out to Loki. Rán can mean robbery in old Norse and perhaps that is what the name is supposed originally to mean, since Rán is the one taking the sailors to their watery death. In Danish 'ran' is another word for stealing.

Rán from me
has taken much,
nor have I
a beloved friend.
My strong son
at last she took –
the worst thing for
my kin and me.
Could
I get revenge with a sword,
with Ægir
it would soon be over.
If
I had hope
of cutting the sea,
against it
I would go to battle.[175]

Is Rán connected to mermaids? That is the question. She does have the same characteristics as mermaids, taking the sailors to their deaths and raising storms. In the saga of Olaf the Holy, we are told he met a mermaid and her sweet song lulled the crew members to sleep:

> When Heilag-Olav was in Viking (Fare I Viking), he met a mermaid who lulled these sailors to sleep with her sweet song and then pulled them down to her in the sea. Above the belt she looked like a woman, below a fish.[176]

The song of the mermaid is always seductive, designed to lull the sailors into a sort of trance and hence to their watery death.

When it comes to the sirens, they were mentioned in ancient Greece as half-birds. In the medieval text *Monstrorum*, mentioned above, we have the first record of a siren described as half-woman, half-fish. The sirens' connection to storms seems to have come from Norse heritage, perhaps because they already knew of the legend of the merman and mermaid called 'hafstramb' and 'margygr'. They are mentioned in *Konungs Skuggsja* (The King's Mirror).

In the medieval period, it is sometimes said that the mermaid was a benevolent creature who warned sailors of bad weather. Perhaps this characteristic is a remembrance of Rán. People would likely have sacrificed to Rán for good weather in the pre-Christian era; therefore, it would not be surprising if people considered her both benevolent and malignant.

In Iceland we have the merman called 'Marbendill', the name being the same in old Norse. The merman mentioned in the *Ladnámabókhe*, a male counterpart to the mermaid, is neither considered evil nor do they do harm to people who happens to catch them in their nets. In the *Ladnámabókhe*:

> Grim went out to fish in the Autumn with his housecarles (servants) and the lad. Thorir lay in the prow and was in a seal-bag which was drawn together at the neck. Grim drew up a mereman and when he came up asked him 'What do you foretell shall be our fortune, or where shall we settle in Iceland?' The merman answered, 'No need to tell the fortune of you and your men, but rather of the lad that lays in the seal bag, he shall there settle and take land where Skalm your mare lays down under her load', and no more words got they from him. Later in the winter Grim and his men rowed out, but the lad was upon land; then the whole crew was lost.[177]

In this example from the Scandinavian area, where water creatures such as the Nixie (Danish – Nykke, Norwegian – Nøkk, Swedish – Näck, Faroe and Icelandic— Nykur) are shapeshifting creatures who can take on various animal figures, we once again see a mention of steel as protection:

> Though he is thus severe only against those who deserve it, yet country people when they are upon the water use certain precautions against his power. Metals, particularly steel, are believed 'to bind the Neck', (binda Necken); and when going on the open sea, they usually put a knife in the bottom of the boat or set a nail in a reed. In Norway, the following charm is considered effectual against the Neck:
>
> Nyk, nyk, naal i vatn! Jomfru Maria kastet staal i vatn! Du sök, äk flyt!
>
> Neck, neck, nail in water! The virgin Mary casteth steel in water! Do you sink, I flit![178]

In an account from Orkney, we have a similar tale of the effect of iron when it comes to sorcery.

> At the Noup-Head in Westra is a rock surrounding with the Sea, call'd Less, which the inhabitants of that Isle say, has this strange propertie – that if a man go upon it, having any Iron upon him (If it were an Iron Nail in his shoe) the Sea will instantly swell in such a tempestuous way, that no boat can come near to take him off, and that the Sea will not be settled till the piece of Iron be flung into it.[179]

Orkney was originally populated by the Norse coming from Norway in the Viking Age, and the culture and folklore of the place would be heavily influenced by Norse beliefs. However, the understanding of the protective effects of iron and steel is not limited to those areas. It was a widespread notion that iron had this effect against Otherworldly beings, witches, and magic in general. It was commonly believed nailing a horseshoe to the door would avert malignant sorcery from beings such as ghosts, witches, or fairies. A strange part about this belief is that the dwarves seem to have no issues working with metal to make weapons, but even they get repelled by iron, if a mortal human throws it into their mound or they are touched by iron. To protect against changelings, an iron scissor would be placed above the cradle to counter fairy magic or a pin of iron or steel would be pinned into babies' clothes to prevent the fairies from switching the child for one of their own.

Finfolk

Finfolk are another kind of shapeshifting being, which seem to be confined to Orkney and Shetland. They can live on land or in water as they please and are powerful sorcerers/sorceresses. According to the legend, Fin males are shaped like human beings but the female is born with a fish tale, like the mermaid, which split into two legs when they come of age. The female of the finfolk want to marry a human. If they do so, they remain seductive beautiful woman, but if they marry a Finman, they turn into ugly hags. So, the females of the finfolk are given much the same attributes as the of mermaids. The finfolk have their own world, called Finfolkaheem, where they live on the ocean bed. Notice the last part of the word 'heem'. In Norse we have 'heim' which means home. Thus, we have a parallel to 'Álfheim', the home of the Álfar, the elves of the Norse world. The finfolk, therefore, likely have their origin in the Norse world, though clearly their description fits with most folklore about mermaids across Europe. The summer home of the finfolk is called 'Hildaland', meaning hidden land. The word Hilda is related to the word Hulda – Huldafólk are also called hidden people, meaning those not visible to the naked eye. The elves and such beings were sometimes called Huldafólk in Iceland and the Faroe Islands. The Huldafólk also look and behave like ordinary people and can on land, as with the finfolk, be hard to distinguish from humans.

Hildaland was an island and could, as with other fairy dwellings, sometimes be seen by humans. The idea of a hidden island has similarities with Avalon from the Arthurian legends. Avalon was a magical island where Arthur recovered and where Excalibur, the magical sword, was forged. Morgan le Fay, Arthur's half-sister's, means 'the fairy'. She was described as a witch and a healer, her attributes being comparable to that of the fairies. The description of Avalon has similarities with the Otherworld of the fairies. Avalon, itself, was ruled by Morgan le Fay and her eight sisters – yet again giving us number nine in relation to the Otherworld and the myths.

Ceasg – The Mermaid with a Salmon tail

Ceasgs are known in Scottish folklore as maidens of the waves (maighdean na tuinne) and they are said to be very beautiful. According to folklore, they lived in streams, rivers, and lakes (lochs) beside the sea and, much like the mermaids, they would be seen with mirrors, combing their long hair. The difference between mermaids and Ceasgs is that the Ceasg possesses the upper body of a beautiful young woman and the lower body of a salmon. The story below is about the Ceasg.

> Once a young crofter was wandering below the cliffs on a beautiful summer night when the wind was still and the silver moon shone through the clear depths of ocean, casting a flood of light through Land-under-Waves. He heard sounds of songs and laughter. He crept softly towards a shadowy rock, and, climbing it, looked down on a bank of white sand. There he beheld a company of mermaids dancing in a ring round a maid who was fairest of the fair. They had taken off their skin coverings, and were gowned in pale blue, and, as they wheeled round about, their copper tresses streamed out behind their backs, glistening in the moonlight. He was delighted by their singing and amazed at their beauty. At length he crept stealthily down the rock and ran towards the skin coverings lying on the sand. He seized one and ran off with

> it. When the mermaids saw him, they screamed and scattered in confusion, and snatching up their skin coverings, they leapt into the sea and vanished from sight. One maid remained behind. This was the fair one round whom the others had been dancing. Her skin covering was gone, and so she could not return to her sea home.[180]

Here the story is much the same as that of the Selkie folk, where the mortal human steals the skin of the mermaid. Hence, we have a mixture of folklore where the beings have similar attributes and properties, and the story goes along the same lines. The colour blue must be symbolic of the ocean, streams, and lakes. But the Ceasg was not always thought to be benevolent. In some stories, the Ceasg swallowed her victims alive.

Mermaid stories can be found across Britain, including Cornwall where they are called merry maids, though their name is rather misleading. Apparently, they can be found at Mermaids' Rock near Lamorna. Here they lure fishermen and sailors to their watery death with their singing. When their song is heard, a ship nearby will sink within seven days.

For example, in small lakes, like Blakemere (or Black mere) near the town of Leek in Staffordshire, England, we are told of a mermaid living there or of her ghost haunting the place. According to folklorist Charlotte S. Burne:

> They say that the mere [Black Mere on Morridge Edge] is fed by a 'blubb' hole from the sea, and moreover that the pool is tenanted by a mermaid. On stormy nights – so the story runs – her wailing cry is heard above the moaning of the wind. Her strange form has been seen gliding over the surface of the dark waters, and woe betide any luckless mortal who chances to pass that way after midnight. [The story of the attempt to drain the pool, and its thwarting, is then told.][181]

According to the local lore, cattle refuse to drink from the pool and birds do not fly over it. It is believed to be a haunted place in general, and several murders are supposed to have taken place at the lake. It's location as a secluded area on the moor likely makes it a bleak place to be, hence the many stories that have sprung up around it.

Another legend about the spot concerns a woman accused of witchcraft by a local man (named Linnet) whose advances she had rejected. Scorned, Linnet convinced the rest of the town that she was a witch whereupon she was taken to the lake, tied up and thrown in for the well-known witch test. If she floated, she was a witch, if she went to the bottom of the lake and drowned, she was innocent. She drowned but witnesses reported that with her dying breath she uttered a curse. Three days later, the man, Linnet, was found dead, chest down in the lake with scars on his face. The locals believed she had turned herself into a water nymph and still haunts the place. As we have noticed before, this mixture of lore is neither uncommon, nor in any way contradictory, as the story simply serves as a warning as to why it is best to stay away from the place.

31

The Kelpies

Kelpies are shapeshifting water creatures, believed to inhabit freshwater lakes and rivers, which may appear in a variety of forms. They are found in Scottish, Welsh, and Irish folklore. However, Yorkshire folklore also has its share of water horses or kelpies, if you will, although the word derives from Gaelic. Water horses or water spirits of various kinds are also found in Norse myth and are similar to those of Scottish kelpies and other water spirits. Although kelpies are Scottish water spirits, they are well known in the rest of Britain as well, and tales of kelpies stretch from Yorkshire and northern England into Cornish folklore.

William Collins mentions the kelpie in his *Ode on the Popular Superstition of the Highlands of Scotland*. A variety of lores surround kelpies, who made themselves particularly attractive to children. If you mount a kelpie, you will find it will take you to the water and drown you because you cannot dismount. At other times, kelpies might frequently appear as men, in particular as hairy humans, who will jump at the mortal to crush him or her to death.

A Dictionary of the Old Scottish Tongue containing the 1674 burgh records for Kirkcudbright, tell us of Kelpie Hoall or Kelpie Hooll, and may be one of the earliest references to kelpie. Numerous Scottish lochs and rivers in Scotland have a kelpie story which has captured many an imagination:

Her travel'd limbs in broken slumber steep,
With drooping willows drest, his mournful sprite
Shall visit sad, perchance, her silent sleep:
Then he, perhaps, with moist and watery hand,
Shall fondly seem to press her shuddering cheek,
And with his blue swoln face before her stand,
And, shivering cold, these piteous accents speak;
'Pursue, dear wife, thy daily toils pursue,

At dawn or dusk, industrious as before;
Nor e'er of me one helpless thought renew,
While I lie weltering on the osier'd shore.
Drown'd by the Kelpie's wrath, nor e'er shall aid thee more!'[182]

In Thomas Lauder's *Tales of the Highlands*, we hear of the author's great uncle who is supposedly so skilled in the art of magic that he can control water spirits or other types of fairies. One evening he as walking beside the Lock-an Dorbe, where he saw a water horse trotting out of the water. In this case the horse was black, a colour often associated with the devil.

> My grand-uncle Macgregor, was so much devoted to the study of that mysterious and unpronounceable art which gives man control over the world of spirits.[183]
>
> Suddenly the black waters of the lake began to heave from their centre without any seeming cause. Not a breath of wind stirred them, yet they came boiling outwards, so as at once to dash their waves on every part of the surrounding shores. A dark object was seen to bound forth upon the beach at no great distance from the spot where Macgregor stood. A less strongly fortified heart would have quailed with fear, but his was armed with potent spells. He stretched his eyeballs towards the object, when, less to his astonishment than delight, he beheld a black horse, of immense size, and of beautiful proportions, approaching him through the lurid twilight. On he came, prancing proudly along the strand, pawing the ground from time to time, and neighing aloud with a voice of thunder, while blue lightning was ever and anon darting from his expanded nostrils, and his eyes were shining like stars. It required not Macgregor's skill to know that this was no ordinary horse, but his superhuman knowledge made him at once aware that it was the water-kelpie himself, and he watched his coming with a heart beating high with hope. Well instructed as to the measures which it now became necessary for him to adopt, he stood aside behind the large stone, and employed certain charms which he knew would aid in his concealment; and as this terrific incarnation of the spirit of the waters was curvetting grandly past him, he sprang suddenly out upon him, and, seizing his bridle with his left hand, he raised aloft his gleaming claymore with his right, and cut it out of the water-kelpie's head at one blow. In an

> instant the terrible spirit was metamorphosed into the shape of a man of huge and very formidable appearance.
>
> 'Give me back my bridle, thou son of earth!' cried he, in a voice like the roaring of a cataract. 'No!' said Macgregor, boldly; 'I have won it, and I shall keep it.'
>
> 'Then', roared the enraged spirit, 'you and it shall never enter your house together!'[184]

By capturing the bridle of the kelpie, he managed to control the spirit. It is believed that you could get it to work for you if you had possession of the bridle, and a better worker you could not have wished for than the kelpie, but if you lost the bridle, you would lose control over the kelpie. We find similar stories in Scandinavia.

The kelpie is mentioned in many of the tales recorded by folklorists, including by Evelyn Blantyre Simpson in *Folklore in Lowland Scotland.*

> It was averred the kelpie (the water sprite) was heard to wail a dirge before it claims a life. Its slogan is one of these sad plaints which the windpipes, and the waters sing, for nature's voice is often raised as an earnest of woe.[185]

Sometimes the kelpie showed itself as a handsome young man who would make love to a human woman. According to Donald A. MacKenzie, girls should be watchful not to fall for its tricks or it will drag her to her untimely death.

> A greatly dreaded demon was the each uisge (Waterhorse), which lived in a loch but never in a stream or river, like our Peallaidh. This demon might assume the form of a handsome young man but could be detected by his horse hoofs and by green water-weeds or sand in his hair. Stories are told of water-horses in human form making love to girls. Some discovered in time the real character of the lower and escaped. Others were taken to the loch and devoured. Children who saw a horse grazing on a green bank mounted it. The demon then rushed into the loch and next day the livers or entrails of its victims were washed ashore.[186]

This has similarities with the 'Åmand' Riverman or the 'Nøkk' or Nixie in Scandinavia as well as from the rest of the Germanic area. In northern Jutland, the 'Åmand' is called the 'Nøkken', thus pointing to either a common origin for these two water spirits or a mixture of the two.

> The 'Åmand' is called 'nøkken' in southern Vendsyssel, south of Vildmosen, because in those areas they use the familiar word «en», but north of Vildmosen the 'Åman' is called 'Nøkki'. There they say «i» as a familiar word, like the Funen people. The name 'Åmand' is a foreign word in Vendsyssel (Northern Jutland). I have never heard it mentioned by a Vendelbo [Person from Northern Jutland], even though I am familiar and have traveled in most parts of Vendsyssel, nor have I heard any other names used for him than 'Nøkken'.
>
> Free schoolteacher A. E. Jakobsen, Örritslev.[187]

The 'Åmand' as well as the Norwegian 'Fosse-Grim' are skilled fiddlers and lure their victims into the water with their enticing music. The same is said about the Nøkk.

> Two boys were playing by the side of the river, and they saw the Stromkarl, or water-spirit sitting in the shore playing his harp. Then the children called out to him and said, 'Stromkarl, why are you playing? There is no salvation for you.' Thereupon the Stromkarl fell to weeping bitterly, threw his harp away, and sank in the deep water. When the boys returned home, they related to their father, who was a godly man, what had befallen them. The father said, 'You have sinned against the Stromkarl, – go back and comfort him and tell him that he too shall be saved.' When they went back to the river, the Stromkarl sat on the shore weeping and lamenting. And the children said, 'Weep not so, Stromkarl, our father says that thy redeemer also liveth.' Then the Stromkarl joyfully took his harp and played sweetly till the sunset.
>
> Jacob Grimm.[188]

You could master the harp by sacrificing to him on a Thursday – 'Torsdag', in Danish, Norwegian and Swedish – which means Thor's day.

According to Evelyn Blantyre Simpson, the kelpie wails a dirge before it claims a life. Similar sounds were said to be heard in places where the 'Åmand' lived. The Nøkk in Scandinavia was said to play the violin, luring their victims to their watery death. The Åmand Riverman was usually male and was said to demand a drowning each year. If he did not receive a sacrifice, you would hear a cry from the river or lake – 'A year has passed but the man has not yet come' – and then shortly after someone would throw themselves into the water and drown. If the Riverman has not received his due, two will drown the next year.

> The man of the river in Odense is rarely seen. There were some people from the countryside who went into the city, and they saw him sitting completely naked on a stone in the river and said: 'The time and the hour have come, but the man has not come'. Before they went home, a man had drowned in the same place.[189]

If you heard the voice, you were bound to be taken by the Riverman. However, if you had a companion such as a dog and reacted fast, you could in some cases save your life by saying 'Not me but the dog', thus, substituting the dog for you as a sacrifice.

It is interesting to find that the folk tales of Yorkshire have clear ties to the Scandinavian lore. A part of the River Ure near Middleham in Wensleydale has such a water horse which is said to demand a drowning each year, just like the Danish 'Åmand' Riverman. Yorkshire was part of the Danelaw where many Danes settled and the yearly drowning correlating exactly with the Danish stories. Thus, this suggests that this part of the story is of Norse origin.

The kelpie, the Riverman and the Nøkk are all water spirits, and the drownings may possibly be a remembrance of pre-Christian religious spectacles where people were sacrificed to the gods. In Tacitus, we hear of how people were drowned in connection with the cult surrounding Nerthus, a female deity. In Odense, there is a superstition that a Riverman sits in the river demanding a drowning each year. The name Odense means Odin's Vi, which in turn means there was a shrine for Odin there at some point and that he was worshipped there. It is known that Odin was one of the deities demanding human sacrifices. We also know that Odin had a connection to horses.

There are also great similarities with the Danish 'Bækhest' and Swedish 'bäckahäst', brook horse, a dangerous Scandinavian water spirit that appeared as a majestic white horse near streams and rivers. According to the Danish Folklorist Evald Tang Kristensen, in Sweden the bäckahäst is a beautiful white horse:

> The Swedes talk about the brook horses. They are white, and when they can get them saddled, they can keep them and make them work for them, and they don't eat anything.[190]

As with the kelpie, it can be made to work for you and it will then do a far better and faster job than an ordinary horse, but you need to be careful, lest it eventually pulls you down into the water.

> A long time ago, there was a girl who was not only pretty but also big and strong. She worked as a maid on a farm by Lake Hjärtasjön in southern Nerike. She was ploughing with the farm's horse on one of the fields by the lake. It was springtime and beautiful weather. The birds chirped, and the wagtails flitted in the girl's and the horse's tracks to pick worms. All of a sudden, a horse appeared out of the lake. It was big and beautiful, bright in colour and with large spots on the sides. The horse had a beautiful mane which fluttered in the wind and a tail that trailed on the ground. The horse pranced for the girl to show her how handsome he was. However, the girl knew it was the brook horse and ignored it. Then the brook horse came closer and closer, and finally he was so close that he could bite the farm horse in the mane. The girl hit the brook horse with the bridle and cried: 'Disappear you scoundrel, or you'll have to plough so you'll never forget it.' As soon as she had said this, the brook horse had changed places with the farm horse, and the brook horse started ploughing the field with such speed that soil and stones whirled in its wake, and the girl hung like a mitten from the plough. Faster than the cock crows seven times, the ploughing was finished, and the brook horse headed for the lake, dragging both the plough and the girl. But the girl had a piece of steel in her pocket, and she made the sign of the cross. Immediately she fell down on the ground and saw the brook horse disappear into the lake with the plough. She heard a frustrated neighing when the brook horse understood his trick had failed. Until this day, a deep track can be seen in the field.[191]

As we have seen, both steel and the sign of the cross is an effective means against the fairies and Otherworldly beings in general, and this one was no exception. She also used the bridle just like the stories from Scotland. Fire was also a powerful protector:

> My grandmother was a midwife and went to Lundbæk a lot, because she had nursed two barons and was so busy with the

> estate. Then the baroness had promised her a bushel of apples, and her husband was to fetch them from Lundbæk. But they were quite heavy for him to carry, and when he came down into the Mill Hole between Grydsted and Hule Mølle, which is an unusually deep hollow road, he came to a horse, and since he was now tired, he thought he could put the sack on it; but still he would not until he had seen it. So, he set fire, and then he saw that it had no head. It slid down the road and drifted past him, and then he went on and came home with his apples.
>
> Jens Mark, Vokslev.[192]

The Danish 'Bækhest' is sometimes headless but its properties are the same as that of the Swedish bäckahäst – and it can bring about your death. Other stories talk of the long horse. The story often starts with young people wanting to go to some party and needing to cross a river or waterway of some sort. Then they see a horse. The first one gets on the horse and the next and the next and each time there is room for one more person at the back of it. Then at the end, when they are in the middle of the water, one of them looks behind him or her and exclaims, 'Oh dear never seen such a long horse'. In that very second, the horse breaks into two and vanishes, leaving the unfortunate partygoers in the middle of the stream. In the worst-case scenario, some have even drowned. However, most of these stories do not have such a dramatic outcome. This tale is closely connected to the lore surrounding the Riverman. Yet again there is no sharp divide separating the lore, they seemingly have all borrowed traits from each other.

In Faroese, Nykur refers to a white-water horse. This is much the same as 'Nøkk' in Northern Jutland in Denmark. Yet again we have the colour white, just like the Swedish 'bäckahäst'.

> The nykur dwells in water; at the bottom, down in the depths, he has his lair; from here he often goes onto land, and it is not good to meet him. Sometimes he is like a beautiful little horse which seems to be good and tame, and thus he lures people to draw near to him to pat him and stroke him along the back. But when they come to touch the tail, they become stuck fast to him, and then he releases no-one, but he drags them with him to the bottom of the water.[193]

Tacitus speaks of white horses kept as flocks who were sacred to the Germanic people. The many stories about the horse in folklore show a line back to the pre-Christian era, perhaps even back to some Indo-European heritage, as we have seen the importance of the horse in their myth and beliefs of Germanic tribes. Besides that, we have seen how water was a liminal space where you could reach the transcendent. In the stories from the folklore there is therefore no doubt we see a remnant of ancient beliefs when it comes to these water spirits.

32

The Ravens

Ravens feature in many cultures – in Ancient Greece they were associated with Apollo, the god of prophecy, the birds being said to symbolise bad luck because of their links to death.

In the Germanic world, ravens were birds of Odin, featuring heavily in connection with battles and devouring the corpses of the slain. Odin's two ravens, Hugin and Munin, were his eyes and ears.

> Hugin and Munin: Odin's Ravens
> Hugin and Munin
> Fly every day,
> Overall, the world;
> I worry for Hugin,
> That he might not return,
> But I worry more for Munin.[194]

Odin's ravens, Hugin and Munin, sit on Odin's shoulder, telling him what they see. Hugin represents memory and Munin, thought. The ravens can be seen as an extension of Odin, or perhaps as his person in another 'Hamr' (body or shape). The ravens may be considered as Odin's helping spirits – you could also say 'familiars'. Odin, himself, was known as the Raven god, named so in *Gylfaginning*:

> Two ravens sit on his shoulders and whisper in his ear all the news they have seen and heard; they are called Hugin and Munin; them he sends forth at dawn to fly through the whole world; they return at prayer time; thus, he gets to know many tidings; therefore, he is called the Raven God; this is how it is called here.[195]

The connection between ravens and the battlefield is also made clear by the involvement of the Valkyries with the ravens:

> Once sorrow had / the Ylfings' son,
> And grief the bride/ who the loved one had borne.
> Quoth raven to raven, /on treetop resting,
> Seeking for food, / There is something I know.[196]

The ravens' connection with the battlefield is driven by their need for food. The name Valkyries means 'chooser of the slain' – they are the ones who select the dead from the battlefield that are to be brought to Valhöll as Einherjar. These were the warriors who had died in battle with honour, and had been found worthy of being classed as the warriors of Valhöll. That said, according to *The Völuspa*, Freya receives half of the fallen:

> The ninth is folksvang, Where Freya decrees.
> Who shall have seats in the hall;
> The half of the dead each day does she choose,
> And half goes to Odin.[197]

The Valkyries are often depicted with connections to ravens because, as we saw above, the ravens devoured the battle-dead.

Ravens are also mentioned in the poem *Beowulf*:

> Stately the hall
> Rose gabled and gilt where the guest slept on
> till a raven black the rapture-of-heaven
> blithe-heart boded. Bright came flying
> shine after shadow.

The Raven Banner

The Raven banner was said to be the emblem of Ragnar Lodbrog and his sons, Cnut the Great and Harald Hardrada, among others. This banner also appears in the Bayeux tapestry. It is said to have been made at midday by Ragnar's three daughters. *The Annals of St. Neots* tells us that the daughters of Ragnar Lodbrog imbued the banner with witchcraft, which spooked the Anglo-Saxons who especially feared the dark witchcraft tainted flags.

> It was said that the three sisters of Hingwar and Hubba (Ivar Boneless and Ubbe), the daughters of Ragnar Lodbrok, had woven that banner and gotten it ready during one single midday's time. Further, it is said that if they were going to win a battle in which they followed that signum, there was to be seen, in the center of the signum, a raven, gaily flapping its wings. But if they were going to be defeated, the raven dropped motionless. And this always proved true.[198]

So, if the banner was waving stiffly in the wind, the battle would be won; if it was hanging down, the battle would be lost.

At the battle of Ashington (AD 1016), Cnut the Great had a raven banner made off white silk.

> a banner which gave a wonderful omen. I am well aware that this may seem incredible to the reader, but nevertheless, I insert it in my veracious work because it is true: This banner was woven of the cleanest and whitest silk and no picture of any figures was found on it. In case of war, however, a raven was always to be seen, as if it were woven into it. If the Danes were going to win the battle, the raven appeared, beak wide open, flapping its wings and restless on its feet. If they were going to be defeated, the raven did not stir at all, and its limbs hung motionless.[199]

The use of ravens on the banner highlights the connection to battle and to victory on the battlefield, and also to Odin, since he was the god of war. In the Orkney sagas, we read about the importance of the banner and how it was widely connected to witchcraft:

> 'Now if you take this banner which I have made for you to the best of my ability, I believe it will prevail as it is carried before. But he who carries it will fall.' The banner was executed with great skill and exquisite workmanship; it was shaped in the form of a raven, and when it waved in the wind it was as if the raven lifted its wings for flight. Earl Sigurd became very angry at his mother's words, and he left the Orkneys with their noble land in return for providing manpower, and then went over to Earl Finleik on Skidamyr. Both parties fielded their manpower; as soon as the battle was under way, Sigurd Jarl's standard-bearer was fatally struck by a shot. The earl ordered another man to carry the banner, and after fighting for

> a while he fell. Three standard-bearers of the earl fell, but he won the victory, and the Orkneys then regained their old lands.[200]

The banners were made to be carried in battle and Earl Sigurd's mother, both a seeress and knowledgeable in sorcery, foretells that the man carrying the banner will fall.

When they arrived in Britain, the Anglo-Saxons and Jutes carried similar beliefs to the Norsemen. Thus, the raven would have figured prominently. In a side chapel window in Newcastle Cathedral, St Oswald is depicted with a raven below his hand. You can wonder what a saint is doing with a raven so placed, but it is very likely connected to his family's past, his parents being Anglo-Saxon and not Christians.

Another, more recent myth, involves the Tower of London and tells that on the day that there are no ravens in the Tower, the kingdom will fall. However, this seems like a relatively new myth, the first reference to the ravens of the Tower dating from 1893. In reality, the Tower ravens can move around freely but their wings are clipped.

According to 'Medievalism, Paganism, and the Tower Ravens', by Boria Sax, the legend that a raven-less Tower will foretell the fall of Britain is only as new as the Second World War.

> In fact, the first references to ravens in the Tower date only from the end of the nineteenth century, while the legend that Britain will fall if the ravens leave the Tower dates only from the end of World War II.[201]

Even though the legend surrounding the Tower is relatively recent, it does not mean a disconnect with the past, as traditional stories are rich with tales involving ravens, including the Germanic stories.

Also, according to folklore, the raven is attracted to a house where there is a corpse, again associating the raven with death:

> Raven: (It is) the belief that the raven is immediately attracted to a house where a corpse is lying.[202]

The same goes for seeing a crow, which is usually meant to be a bad omen. In the *Folklore of Herefordshire* there is a story about a man who sees a white crow following him home:

> ... farmer at Longtown was ploughing and was surprised to see a white crow come perch near his plough; When he came home at night the bird followed him and hovered about near his house. He went in and told his wife, remarking 'That's not for nothin' its all up wi' me afore long.' The next night he was poisoned by a lodger in his house, who was afterwards hanged for the murder.[203]

Denmark has a creature called the 'Valravn', the raven of the fallen. Val comes from the Norse word 'the fallen' which is combined with 'raven.' We find similar wording in 'Valhöll' and the 'Valkyries'. In Danish folklore the 'Valravn' is often half wolf and half eagle or raven. In folksong, it is sometimes known as the wild raven and is a knight that has been transformed into a raven. How this story came about and whether it was a knight that became a raven or a raven that became a human is unclear. In some stories, it seems that perhaps the raven ate the fallen on the battlefield and thus could become a human/knight due to sorcery – but it could only walk at night. For it to fully transform back into a human, a human sacrifice in the form of a male child was needed.

In the Danish folk song, raven is the name of a mythical creature in the form of a man who has been transformed into a raven. The curse can only be broken if he drinks the blood of an infant. The raven is known from the Danish medieval song tradition, appearing in nine known versions of the same song.

> If they did not find and bury the king or the chieftain in a battle, ravens came and ate him, and these ravens became Valravni, and the one who ate his heart gained human understanding and could do evil and deceive people and had superhuman power, and they were some terrible animals.
> Peder Johansen, Mos sø.[204]

The raven was to target the king or chieftain. Odin was worshipped by the kings and chieftains and many of them claimed descent from him – one such noble family was the Ulfeldt, one of the very old Danish noble families. The ravens were Odin's bird, so you could say the folklore of the 'Valravn' comes full circle. Ravens were believed to be wise birds and had many connections in folklore, both in Germanic and Celtic lore.

Another story from Evald Tang Kristensen tells how the souls from a shipwreck transformed into birds, pointing to the importance of shapeshifting as a factor in the deceased's passage to the Otherworld or the world of the dead:

> Once upon a time a ship was stranded on the shore of Bunken Beach, and much wrong was done to it. Part of the prow remained in the quicksand on the shore. In bad weather, a bird comes and sits on the wreck, but flies away screaming out over the sea in the direction the ship was destined to sail. These are the souls of the shipwrecked who now have the form of birds.[205]

In Yorkshire, parents threatened badly-behaving children with the prospect of ravens carrying them away, again underscoring ravens' connection to death. In many places in Britain, the raven was connected to the devil; despite this, the raven was still a bird people deeply respected.

33
Trees

Trees have a prominent position in folklore and myth across the world, and also a central function in many religions. In the Garden of Eden, we have the tree of life along with the tree of knowledge of good and evil. Christians also see the tree of life as a symbol of the cross.

In Germanic tradition, the first humans, Askr and Embla, were created from trees, The name Askr literally means ash tree. Also, the tree of life in the Norse world was a giant ash. Embla was created from an elm.

Both in Britain and Scandinavia we find the idea of a birth tree. In legend, King Arthur comes to the court of Gorlagon, the werewolf king, who tells a story about a king whose life is tied to a tree growing from the hour of his birth. Similarly, we find in Scandinavian lore a tree being planted when a child is born. The child will grow stronger as long as the tree does. Such a tree was never to be cut down lest it hurt the child whose life was connected to it.

Many would make offerings to the tree, including little pieces of clothing, hoping their wishes would come true. Often planted near farms, the tree was believed to have protective properties.

Therefore, it is unsurprising to find similar beliefs in the folklore of ordinary people across centuries. Many trees or plants continued to be sacred in some way and were believed to have healing or magical properties. Here is a selection of some of the most prominent ones.

Oak

As we have seen, the Germanic tribes worshipped their gods in groves and had sacred trees, one of those being the Oak of Donar, at an unknown location some place in Hesse, Germany. Victims of sacrifice were hung in oak trees in the Germanic world, and it was believed that Thor preferred this tree in particular.

The oak tree was one of those trees believed to be a fairy tree in which the fairies could live and around which they would dance. In Denmark, it was known as a troll tree due to the crooked branches it often grew. As in Britain, the oak was associated with the various Otherworldly beings. Prominent in British folklore is the notion that the oak could grant you a wish if you walked around, it three times.

> A woodman went to the forest to fell some timber: Just as he was applying the axe to the trunk of a huge oak out jumped a fairy, who beseeched him with the most supplicating gestures to spare the tree. Moved more by fright and astonishment than anything else, the man consented, and as a reward for his forbearance was promised his fulfilment of his three next wishes.[206]

In this tale from Thomas Sternberg, we have the oak as a fairy tree. We also find the number three, one of those significant numbers in folklore, in Christianity, and in the old beliefs prior to Christianity.

In Herefordshire, an ash tree growing out of a stump of a former oak, was revered as a healing tree:

> In Oaker Coppice, Eyton, is a curious ash tree growing out of the stump of an oak. Its trunk is covered with hairs, small lockes of human hair placed in notches made in bark. Eyton folk believe that offering of child's hair to this tree will cure the cough, and an old keeper stated that people from Eyton living in London had sent him locks of hair, requesting him to fasten them in the bark of the tree, which he had done.[207]

Such traditions involved not just hair but also pieces of clothing or rags given as tokens to the tree. In Denmark similar traditions surrounded healing or hollow trees.

> Just as there are also several specific beech trees, where one could seek healing, there are also several oak trees that were hollow trees. One such was found in Ebberup (Denmark), west of Skjoldnæsholm. Its trunk was split, and it was often sought for healing. People liked to leave some pieces of their clothes (rags) as an offering to the tree.[208]

Likewise, if a child lost a baby tooth, that tooth would be put into the tree. Then the child would get strong adult teeth. Moreover, people with wounds could rub some of the discharge matter into the trunk, resulting in a healing wound.

> Cutting three furrows crosswise in the tree and rubbing a little matter into the wounds is also said to have a healing effect, as it is believed that the tree will take the disease in the place of the sick person, just as it would when the clothes would eventually rot.[209]

It is not surprising that it is the oak tree which is positioned as a healing tree since Thor was connected to this tree and, as we have seen, he was connected to prosperity, good weather and protection. So, it is therefore not a great leap to think Thor would be linked to healing. Indeed, in Britain oak was used in medical remedies.

In Scandinavia, as we have touched above, the oak tree, or perhaps the Beech was frequently called a hollow tree, believed to have very special powers. Branches of these trees would have grown together to form a hole which could be crawled through, or a young sapling might be split in the middle to form a hole a patient, perhaps a child, could be pulled through. As the tree was healing the notion was that the patient would also heal. These trees were thought to cure various diseases, such as rickets.

This practice was associated with various rituals that occurred on certain days of the year. The most powerful time was at midnight during the first new moon of the year. Some trees were active only in midsummer, at midnight on June 23. If the moon was full, the result would be better. At the same time, the best result would be on Thursdays, the day of Thor. The patient had to be pulled through first one way and the other, but it was important that it was in the right order because otherwise the result could be the opposite.

During some rituals, the other participants either had to sing or dance around the tree. Rituals differ from tree to tree and from region to region. In some cases, the ritual had to be repeated three or nine times. All this was probably a legacy from Pagan eras.

> It was thought to bring good luck to carry an acorn in your pocket, or if you had diarrhoea you could grate a ripe acorn into warm milk and give to the patient, just as remedies made from oak were used as a medical remedy against sore shoulders on horses. You boiled the bark and then washed the sores with the water.[210]

Carrying an acorn in your pocket was thought to bring good luck. Sore shoulder on horses could be treated medically with an oak potion – you boiled the bark and then washed the sores with the water.

The wishing Cork Oak tree in the Devon village of Coombe-in-Teignhead is a good example of what was thought of these trees. Legend has it that it brought good luck as well as having healing properties. The beliefs surrounding this tree are explained in the *Oxford Dictionary of Plant Lore*. There, a Christmas card entry tells us that this has been a wishing tree for 350 years, dating back to the great plague, when people came to walk around the tree three times, making a wish. This could be for good health or something entirely different. If obtaining a piece of the cork from this tree, a similar ritual could be held at home, making the piece of the tree the important part of the ritual, not the place. We notice yet again that you had to walk around the tree three times for the ritual to work.

The oak was also connected to the weather, with familiar rhymes such as:

> If an oak is out before the ash
> There will be a splash [fine summer]
> If the ash is out before the oak
> There will be a soak [wet summer].[211]

Connection with the weather is once again unsurprising since the oak was Thor's tree, the god of thunder and the weather.

The following witchcraft case from the very small town of Guldager in North Jutland, Denmark, confirms the notion that a tree could contain magic. It also demonstrates a degree of tolerance on the part of the authorities at that time.

The case, which took place at Børglum from 1576–1577 is somewhat special, and yet it accords with the law and its conduct is very typical of witch trials in Denmark. The land register itself is a little damaged, preventing us from reading all of it, but there is enough to gain a picture of events. Apparently, an oak had been put on Laurs Laursen's property, which means someone either planted a tree on his land or placed an oak branch close to his house.

The case begins with a suspicion that some sort of witchcraft has been deployed, which Laurs Laursen believes is to blame for his stepson, Laurs Knudsen's illness. Following Laurs's inquiry, a Karen Ibsdatter (Ib's daughter) testifies that it was a Maren Olufs, who gave her the oak. What is very interesting here is that 'Putting an oak on' is not a wording seen elsewhere in the witch trials of Denmark. Inquiries were made to various places, including the Hex

Museum (Museum of Witchcraft of Denmark), but none have heard this kind of phrase before. What we do know is that the oak was believed to be a troll tree and a tree with magical properties and a healing tree. Which is probably why Laurs Laursen believed it connected to witchcraft.

You can read this in *Danish Trees in Legend and Beliefs*:

> With the tree, one was faced with a being who, on his own power, could take on diseases and free the sick from them.[212]
>
> If you suffered from arthritis, you could go to an oak tree at midnight, embrace it silently, then look up at the top and say, 'Here I stand, oak! I will send all my arthritis to you. Here you stand, me passing. In the name of God, the Father, the Son, and the Holy Spirit'.[213]

The patient should never again approach this tree. If others cut into the tree, they risked getting arthritis or other deposited diseases. According to folklore, witchcraft was not in itself harmful. The problem was the intention behind it. It follows that what could benefit, namely white sorcery, could also be turned into malign sorcery. In the case of this oak, it is likely to have been healing tree which was not to be cut down or removed. If a person put such a tree on another person's property without mentioning that it was a healing tree, the risk was that the other person would cut down or remove the tree and might thereby be affected by disease or sorcery.

In this case, no one seemed to consider 'Putting an oak on', to be an odd phrase, so it must have been a known term. You can therefore say that some trees continued to be sacred up through the Christian era. Naturally, beliefs changed over time, but there is no doubt that the Pagan beliefs continued to live prosperously side by side with the official faith, Christianity. The tree or the spirit of the tree, the Vætr, could both be beneficial if you gave respect, but at the same time it also had to be handled with caution.

When people were executed because they committed atrocities or malign deeds, they were not buried in consecrated ground but at a crossroads. But it was thought that these people may not rest in their graves, so in order for the living not to be haunted by these malign apparitions, precautions had to be taken. One way to do this was to pin the body to the ground with an oak stake. This could avert sorcery, and it would also prevent the undead from rising from the grave. In Denmark, a similar way of banning a ghostly apparition from rising from their grave was to drive a pole through the spot where it was believed the person was buried. A person who could not rest in the grave was said to become a night raven.

> There is no doubt that the self-murderer, or the doer of some atrocious deed of violence, murder, or lust, was buried by some lonely roadside, in a road-crossing, or by the wild woodside, and that the oak or, oftener, thorn stake was driven through his breast; but not because of any intended scorn, or horror, or abhorrence. These were the characters who – to use an expression common enough among us to this day, though perhaps we do not trouble to think of its origin or meaning – could not 'rest in their graves'. They will to wander, nay, often they were self-constrained to wander about the scenes of their crimes, or the places where their unhallowed carcases were deposited, unless, that is to say, they were prevented; and as they wanted the semblance, the simulacrum, the-shadow-substance of their bodies for that purpose – otherwise there could have been no appearance – the body it was which was made secure by pinning it to the bottom of the grave by aid of the driven stake.[214]
>
> An old priest in Emmerlev by Höjer, [Denmark] named Holst is said to have told the confirmation candidates that those who are under the spell sometimes take on the form of a night raven and fly around in the air. The stake had left a large hole in the right wing. If it so happens that someone sees the sun through this hole, he could then see everything that was otherwise hidden from the eyes of others.[215]

In other stories, if you looked through the hole in the wing you would become insane, much like you do when touched by the magic of fairies or elves.

The Ash Tree

To the Norse, the ash tree was the tree of life itself – Yggdrasil. Therefore, this would also be the case for the Anglo-Saxons when they arrived in Britain. In time, like the oak, this tree therefore became a fairy tree. The ash was at the centre of the May Pole dance, being cut down on the May Day morning and then adorned with ribbons and flowers.

The Danes usually used the oak tree as a hollow tree where they pulled the sick children through, and this was also the case with ash trees in many places in Britain.

> A remarkable instance of the extraordinary superstition which still prevails in the rural districts of Somerset has lately come to light at Athelney. It appears that a child was recently born in that neighborhood with a physical ailment, and the neighbors persuaded the parents to resort to a very novel method of charming away the complaint. A sapling ash was split down the center, and wedges were inserted so as to afford an opening sufficient for the child's body to pass through without touching either side of the tree. This having been done, the child was undressed, and, with its face held heavenward, it was drawn through the sapling in strict accordance with the superstition. Afterwards the child was dressed, and simultaneously the tree was bound up. The belief of those who took part in this strange ceremony is that if the tree grows the child will grow out of its bodily ills. The affair took place at the rising of the sun on a recent Sunday morning in the presence of the child's parents, several of the neighbours, and the parish police-constable.[216]

The child was from that day on connected to this very tree, so if it was cut down the child would suffer deteriorating health (or even death) as the sapling needed to grow strong so the child would as well. This idea is similar to the idea that when a tree was planted in connection with a child's birth, the tree and the child would remain connected. The life source of the child was linked to the spirit on the tree. This reaffirms the belief in animism, where everything in nature has its own spirit.

A shrew ash in Richmond Park was a tree revered as a healing tree.

> The Shrew Ash was a very ancient, gnarled tree near Sheen Gate which, not uncommonly for ash trees, had a reputation for curing sick infants and animals. Mothers would bring children with whooping cough and other ailments to the tree to take part in a secret dawn ritual led by a 'shrew mother,' or 'priestess,' or 'witch'. The ritual involved passing the child over and under a 'witchbar', a wooden bar wedged into the tree, while the 'shrew mother' muttered or sang verses, timing her recitation so that a particular word coincided with the first of the sun's rays. If the charm didn't work, it could be blamed on mistiming.[217]

The shrew mother or witch would be a wise woman who knew how to perform this ritual, among others. It was very important for the ritual to be performed correctly. It was common practice to use wise men and women to perform these rituals or to give advice in the matter of malign sorcery or illness. The sad thing is that these wise men and women were then sometimes accused of malign magic themselves, but they were nevertheless sought out to help with various issues. In the case below, from Denmark, a wise woman takes care of the ritual to make sure it is performed correctly.

> In Selshausdal Forest by Lake Tissø is a tree whose branches have grown together so much that a house has been formed in the trunk. The tree was still standing in 1876 and was still used for diseases. One Thursday night at 12:00 it was used to pull children through this hole in the tree. An old woman lived near the tree. She knew how the ritual worked and usually she received 3 marks for her inconvenience. She put the child through the opening three times and each time she walked around the tree three times (from right to left and read a reading that no one understood).[218]

As again with the number three, walking the wrong way around the tree whilst saying a rhyme is a common feature in these rituals. Perhaps having to do something backwards was a way for humans to enter into a sort of liminal space of the Otherworld or non-Christian world. To give an example, the advice for getting dressed to avoid sorcery was to start by taking on the right sleeve first, and the same with stockings or pants. This way you were still in accordance with the good Christian way and thus protected. However, when performing sorcery, you stepped into another realm outside of the Church and doing things backwards was a common theme.

Burning ash leaves was a way to treat various ailments – for example, you could treat ringworm by letting the smoke surround the affected body part. Similarly, ash was used to keep malign sorcery away. Cutting a branch from an ash tree could also give you bad luck, which of course is a little contradictory considering burning an ash branch gave good luck and kept evil spirits away. But there need not be any logic to folklore.

> A man cut a slip from an ash-tree growing near a fairy dwelling. On his way home in the evening, he stumbled and fell. He heard the fairies give a laugh at his mishap. Through the night he was hoisted away and could tell nothing of what happened till in the morning he found himself in the byre, astride on a cow, and holding on by its horns.[219]

As we have seen, the ash tree is a fairy tree, and offending the fairies could end badly. Cutting a bit off a fairy tree, just like digging into a fairy mound, could be considered offensive to the fairies who would take revenge.

Rowan

The rowan tree, also called mountain ash, held a prominent place in folklore, especially in Scotland. Both the ash tree and the rowan tree had a prominent position among the Danes and the Norsemen. In Britain, this tree was particularly important in Scottish folklore and was believed to have held magical properties – it supposedly protected you from witchcraft, enchantments and Otherworldly beings such as elves and trolls, ghosts and any other beings thought to do harmful magic.

> They plant rowan outside their house for protection in Scotland. When my parents moved into their house in Harrow, where I still live, in AD 1938, my father planted a Rowan sapling in the garden – it was a new house. He brought the sapling from Scotland; He didn't really believe, but he did it to keep up the custom.[220]

The rowan and its branches could be used as protective charms.

There are, throughout Ireland, stories of milk stealing and butter bewitching and there are many tales of butter being taken from the milk, and consequently of many an antidote of how to prevent this. Witches and Otherworldly beings were thought to steal the butter luck or the butter itself, and a placement of a rowan branch would protect the production. Another way was to tie a rope with *nine* knots in it around the churn – this would bring the butter back if it had been stolen. As a preventative measure you could put a harrow-pin and a crooked sixpence in the four corners of the house. Another common method was to place a half-burnt turf under the churn, or a piece of heather, or a branch of rowan-berries (mountain ash) was said to be effective.

Once, in the parish of Fenagh, there was a family whose supply of milk invariably turned sour, and no butter was to be obtained. It chanced that there came to them one day an old traveller who asked for a drink. 'Well', said the woman of the house, 'I cannot give you milk, for all we have is bad'. 'How is that?' said the traveller. So, he was told all they knew about the matter:

> 'If you give me a lodging this night', said he, 'I will get your butter back for you'; and thinking things could not be much worse, they let him remain.
>
> After sunset the traveller barred every door and window in the place, and made a great fire of turf, and in the fire, he placed nine irons. Now, as the irons got hot, a loud roaring was heard without, and an old woman who dwelt near was seen beating at the door and windows and shouting to be let in.
>
> 'Take the irons from the fire, they have me burnt!' she said. But the traveller answered that until she brought back the butter she had taken, the irons would remain in the fire to burn her. Then she tore round the house in a fury, and got upon the roof to try and get in that way to take the irons from the fire; but finding it was useless, she went home, roaring all the time for the pain she was in, and brought the butter in a barrel to the door, upon which the irons were taken from the fire, and she was released. From that time the family had no cause to complain of their milk.[221]

As we have seen, iron was efficient against sorcery, and the number nine is a common element to these tales. A similar story of stealing butter luck is found in the once Danish area of Yorkshire:

> He took the heart of one of the animals which had died under the malevolent witch's maleficent practices, and having provided himself with all the various requisites, proceeded to stick it carefully with nine new pins, nine new needles, and nine new nails. Then a fire was to be made as the midnight hour, that time of the night [the depth of the night] drew on, yet not with ordinary or any haphazard kind of fuel; but with bottree wood – in one or two of the stories rowan-tree wood, or even ash-wood, was specified – and such wood only was to be used. And the fire was to be kindled and kept up so that there might be the hottest possible bed of bright, clear-burning embers exactly at midnight. But before lighting the fire all the doors and windows of the house were to be made fast, very safely fast; and besides, the utmost care had to be taken to darken the windows, and even cover the cracks in the door (if there were any), so that no ray of light should by any possibility be seen from the outside.[222]

In *Smaatræk fra Vestfyn* (Small Stories from Westerns Funen, Denmark) in 1922, you can read tales about witches and wise people in the area. Here, we are told of a farm where they could not get butter in the kernel and the cows were sick. A wise man was summoned. The first thing he did was to tip the content of a Jutland pot (a kettle) over the hearth. Fire is also very effective against witches and Otherworldly beings:

> 'Now the witchcraft was rendered powerless', he said, 'but if you want to see who the witch is, you should just go into the neighboring farm and see what they were up to'. The farmer went into the neighbor's farm, and here he found both the wife and daughter sitting with a sheet over them. They were in the process of milking another man's cows through an awl in the ceiling.[223]

As with Scotland, the witch will come to the house when the iron is burning her. You can burn the witch by throwing the iron into the fire (and in this story the cream).

> When one cannot churn butter, then they have the power of the cream, then a horseshoe must be made in the devil's name and thrown in, or the cream in the same name is thrown into the oven and burned; if anyone comes to the door, then it is the witch who has taken the butter.[224]

On the eve of Walpurgis (April 30), a rowan is placed at all doors and over the roof of carriages to prevent witches from entering and from riding away with the cows.[284] It was believed that on this night, witches travelling to the Great Sabbath would steal cows to ride on. They would gathered ingredients for their witches' brew this very night, as they were believed to be more potent at this time. The placement of rowan branches at the house and at the stable entrance protected both the household and the livestock. If you had brooms made of rowan, you could turn your brooms upside down on this night, placing them at building entrances.

> May eve the farmer sticks a piece of mountain ash in their crop, that way the fairies would not take the luck of the crop.
>
> One may eve the farmer cuts rowan berry in the shape of a ring and ties to the cow's tail with red string. It was an old belief that butter would be taken off the milk if rowan berries was not tied to the cows' tale.[225]

Beyond this, rowan was generally considered a magical tree, and the power of the rowan was even more potent if you could find 'Flyverøn' (flying rowan), which was self-sown in cracks or crevices in rocks or other trees, as a consequence of birds dropping rowan berries mid-flight.

The use of rowan wood is also mentioned in the story about the Laidley Worm of Spindlestone Heugh. According to the Northumberland Archives, it was first written down in 1778: 'The legend of a dragon stalking the countryside of Northumberland is first recorded by William Hutchinson in 1778. Hutchinson was given the ballad by the Reverend Robert Lambe of Norham who was almost certainly involved in its composition. Despite Lambe's claims of transcribing an ancient manuscript, it seems he took inspiration from local songs and stories which themselves may have been localized version of ballads found in Scotland and Iceland'.[226]

> I weird yebe a laidly worm,
> And borrowed shall ye never be,
> Until Childe Wynd, the king's own son,
> Come to the heugh and thrice kiss the;
> Until the world comes to an end,
> Borrowed shall ye never be.[227]

'Worm' in old English means serpent or dragon, and the serpent or dragon of medieval times that often dripped poison, rather than the fire spewing dragon we think of today.

In the story a Saxon Princess is cursed by her stepmother and turns into a dragon. She is unable to be rescued or returned back into her human form until her brother comes and kisses her three times. Besides the fact it's her brother rather than a lover who liberates her, the story follows the usual template of a fairytale. Childe Wynd, the brother, builds a ship with a keel of rowan wood. When the evil stepmother raises a storm against him with witchcraft, the rowan keel protects him. In the same story Childe Wynd, when returning to Bamburgh, touches his stepmother with a rowan twig turning her into a toad.[228]

The stepmother being turned into a toad is interesting, as that is one of the creatures the witch is known to favour, along with the hare and the cat. The toad emphasises the witch's malign nature. According to the story, the witch remains bad until she too has received three kisses. The rowan twig breaks the witch's ability to do magic while protecting the wielder of the rowan twig against the sorcery.

The Elder Tree

The elder tree is both feared and revered in British folklore, being both a fairy tree and a tree of witches. But in Britain, beliefs surrounding this tree are slightly ambivalent. In some places, it is considered unlucky to carry around something from the elder tree:

> Elder – unlucky to bring either flowers or wood into the house: (a) because it is the witches' tree, (b) because it was believed that Judas Iscariot hanged himself from an elder tree, (c) because if you fall asleep under elder flowers the scent will poison you or you will never wake up.[229]

In some places, planting an elder tree near the house was considered good luck. Perhaps this all depends on location. For instance, on the Isle of Man:

> Each old cottage has a 'trammon', or elderberry tree, outside the door. This is used by the 'Phynodderree' to swing on. He is a kind of faun who can bring much luck and even help materially in outside work.[230]

It was also said that if you burned elder wood, you would become bewitched. This makes sense since it is a witch tree, and it was unlucky to have it in your garden. However, there are also stories where it is said to be safe to take flowers, berries, and branches from the elder tree, but only if you ask permission.

The idea of burning an elder tree is seen in Danish folklore as well; however, also in Denmark it is cautioned against burning the elder tree in certain cases:

> Elderwood must not be burned while geese and ducks are incubating, because then you will not have success with the fry.[231]

If you were to take something from the elder tree you had to ask for permission:

> This was something quite new to me, and the clue seemed worth following up. So coming home I went straight down to my back yard, where old Johnny Holmes was cutting up firewood – chopping kindling, as would have said. Watching the opportunity, I put a knot of elderwood in the way and said, 'You are not feared

> of chopping that are you?' 'Nay' he replied at once, 'I bain't feared of choppin' he bain't wick (alive) but if her were wick I dussn't, not without axin' the old gal's leave, not if it were ever so.... [the words to be used are] Oh, them's slape enuff, you just say 'owd gal, give me thy wood, and oi wome of moine, when I graws inter tree'.[232]

The Danish story is very similar. The elder tree was thought to be a healing tree, housing a creature called an Elder Mother or elder woman. You were to treat the tree with respect, and if you wanted to use something from the elder tree, you would have to ask permission. You would thus have to say three times: 'elder mother, elder mother, elder mother, give me some of your wood, then I will give you some of mine'. If you did not ask for permission, all kinds of accidents could afflict the person who had felled or taken something from the tree. The wording of the British tale – 'Give me some of yours and I will give you some of mine' – is the same, almost to the letter, as the Danish saying. The tales do not specify exactly who lives in the elder tree. In Denmark, a fairy/elven woman lives in the tree and she was believed to be the goddess Freya. But once you had asked permission to use some of the elder tree, its healing properties were potent:

> To remove abscesses, knots, tars, etc. on people and cattle you use the following form and procedure: There is an abscess there, I thought it had become something, but it did not, now I put it on this stone there. Pooh, pooh, pooh! This is read three times while placing the three front fingers of the right hand around the place in question and moving them for each sentence to a different point in the circle which you form around the abscess; they can be moved both back and forth. During the last sentence, you spit three times on the fingers and put them down against the stone that is to receive the disease, and which must be placed in such a way that no one crosses it, preferably under a tree. The elder tree was specially mentioned.[233]

Several elements in this story offer a good example of what people believed. As well as treating abscesses, warts could also be cured:

> They say warts can be removed by rubbing them with a Green elder sticke and then burying the sticke to rot in Mucke.[234]

If you ate the elderflower fried in butter at midsummer, you would not get a fever that year. If you had a fever, you could tie a ribbon that you had worn in bed around an elder branch during the waning moon. Here again, is the notion that a tree could take on diseases.

Many other plants and trees were important in folklore, but this is a good demonstration of how trees continued to be sacred. The idea that nature was spirited, as with pre-Christian animism, continued into the Christian era among the common people, and folklore preserved, in transformed ways, the old beliefs associated with sacred groves.

34

Black Spectral Dogs in Folklore, the Barghest

The black dog in British folklore is usually a hellhound, but this fiend is also seen elsewhere in Europe. The animal is normally described as an unusually large shapeshifting dog with glowing red demonic blazing eyes, although the eye colour can also be yellow. Either way, encountering such a beast would surely have been a frightening experience. The Baskerville hound which features in the Sherlock Holmes fictional stories demonstrates this kind of dog and is a good illustration of the importance of this sort of apparition in English folklore. As is the nature of folklore, there are no clear-cut lines defining the various beasts and their characteristics. Some of these spectral dogs can shapeshift into horses, donkeys, goats, pigs, or other such beasts, even a headless man. The common theme in the tales is that they are omens of death or that they can do people bodily harm.

This apparition goes under different names including Barghest, Gytrash and Patfoot in Yorkshire, and Old Shuck in East Anglia. Often, these spectral canines are associated with watery places, dangerous ravines, bridges, undersides or churchyards, dark places associated with death. Sometimes the apparition was believed to be a human who has committed some evil deed and who restlessly wanders the earth haunting the living. That these hell hounds are connected to waters and wells of various kinds is also not surprising, given the pre-Christian links to these liminal spaces, that continued into the Christian era. That it became a fiend, or a dog linked with the devil is not surprising either as the old beliefs became associated with the devil.

The Barghest is reckoned to haunt Troller's Gill in the Yorkshire Dales along with some Scandinavian trolls who throw rocks at the unsuspecting traveller. The Reverend Thomas Parkinson, writing in 1888, explains:

> In the whole of this neighbourhood, belief in the bargest, or spectre hound, has held a prominent place in popular superstition

> and folklore. The usual form assumed by this apparition was (is?) that of a large dog, with long hair, immense eyes, large as saucers and bright as fire. Often he dragged with him, fixed to his feet, or round his neck, a chain, whose clanking, in the stillness and darkness of night, added much to the terror which he inspired. Many are the places he 'haunted,' and many are the legends of his appearance; but one of his favorite spots was the dark Troller's Gill.

Howling dogs are considered a bad omen. This is also the case in Danish folklore:

> When dogs howl, an accident is imminent in the house.[235]

The Barghest and other such apparitions also have similarities with the 'Helhest' Hel-horse, 'Gravso' Grave Sow, and 'Kirkelam' Church Lamb, in Danish folklore, which are animals that were buried in churchyards as sacrifices to protect the church building and grounds. In Denmark, dogs were buried alive in the Viking Age and after on the threshold of stables, to ward off evil of various kinds.

Church Grims often appeared as black dogs, but could also come in various other shapes, such as pigs, lambs, and horses. Some indicators suggest that British folklore involving this fiend might come from the Anglo-Saxon period as the name might derive from the German 'berg-geist' (Mountain-Spirit) or 'Bär-geist' (Bear-Spirit). Another suggestion for the meaning of the name is 'Bahr-geist' (funeral beer).

In a local ballad recorded by William Hime in 1827, we are told what the unfortunate traveller who confronts or happens to lock eyes with this apparition would expect:

> A dreadful thing from the cliff did spring,
> And its wild bark thrilled around.
> Its eyes had the glow of the fires below
> 'Twas the form of the spectral hound.

In this story, a man calls out the demon dog at Troller's Gill and the next morning his dead body is found with marks not made by mortal men. In this case the apparition is not just an omen of impending death but actively causes the man's death, after he confronts the fiend.

Spectral dogs can be found in different places such as ravines, crossroads, bridges, churchyards and stretches of roads often near water. In East Anglian folklore, the story of Black Shuck is connected to a storm:

> If this were a stormy night instead of a stormy day the old fisher-folk of the coast would say it were just the time for Black Shuck to be abroad; for he revels in the roaring of the waves and loves to raise his awful voice above the howling of the gale. Black Shuck is the 'Moddey Dhoo' of the Norfolk coast. He takes the form of a huge black dog, and prowls along dark lanes and lonesome field footpaths, where, although his howling makes the hearer's blood run cold, his footfalls make no sound. You may know him at once, should you see him, by his fiery eye; he has but one, and that, like the Cyclops, is in the middle of his head. But such an encounter might bring you the worst of luck: it is even said that to meet him is to be warned that your death will occur before the end of the year.[236]

As with the other spectral dogs, Black Shuck comes out at night, and the common trait is the prediction of ill omens. That a specific person who has committed evil deeds is connected to the apparitions of the hellhound is also a trait seen regularly. In some cases, the dog is seen near execution sites or by crossroads, which were liminal spaces and connected to witches.

In York, a Barghest in the shape of a black pig was seen after the execution of the witch Mary Bateman in 1809. At Hergest Court, Herefordshire, it is connected to a man named Black Vaughan:

> Hergest court was, or perhaps still is, haunted by a demon dog, said to have belonged to Black Vaughan, and to have accompanied him during his life. It is seen before a death in the Vaughan family. A native of Kington writes, – 'In my young days I knew of people who lived at Hergest court well, and they used to tell be strange things of the animal. How he inhabited a room at the top of the house, which no one ever ventured to enter; how he was heard there at night, clanking his chain; how at times he was seen wandering about (minus the chain). His favorite haunt was a pond, the watering place on the high road from Kington. The spot was much dreaded, and if possible, avoided by late travelers. I knew many who said they had seen the 'Black dog of hergest'.[237]

The black dog in this story is connected to death and to the restless soul of Black Vaughan, warning of deaths in this family. Its haunt is a pond near Kington, once again a connection to water.

It seems to have been impossible to avoid such an omen. According to the Reverend Atkinson, a story is connected to the church of St Hildas. A Barghest is haunting the area nearby, late at night, and a young man wandering home drunk encounters the fiend. For him to escape the Barghest, which in this case is in the shape of a donkey, he enters the churchyard. He tries to evade the apparition by crossing the churchyard, but all is in vain. In the end he tumbles down into a grave and breaks his neck.

The Gytrash, in the Yorkshire area, is another name for the Barghest. This particular one would sometimes appear as a horse, which yet again fits with the church Grim in Scandinavia, which is often a horse.

> As this horse approached, and as I watched for it to appear through the dusk, I remembered certain of Bessie's tales, wherein figured a North-of-England spirit called a 'Gytrash', which, in the form of horse, mule, or large dog, haunted solitary ways, and sometimes came upon belated travelers, as this horse was now coming upon me. It was very near, but not yet in sight; when, in addition to the tramp, tramp, I heard a rush under the hedge, and close down by the hazel stems glided a great dog, whose black and white colour made him a distinct object against the trees. It was exactly one form of Bessie's Gytrash – a lion-like creature with long hair and a huge head [...], with strange pretercanine eyes [...]. The horse followed, – a tall steed [...]. Nothing ever rode the Gytrash: it was always alone [...].[238]

At other times, the Gytrash would be seen as a donkey, and of course as a black demonic dog, thus again demonstrating there are no clear lines by which the shapes of these fiends were precisely defined.

> Old Trash is considered a certain death-sigh and has obtained the local names of 'Trash' or 'Striker'. He generally appears to the family from which death is about to select this victim and is more or less visible according to the distance of the event. The Barghaist has assumed the form of a white cow or a horse but on occasions Trash is described as having the appearance of a large dog, with very broad feet, shaggy hair, dropping ears, and

> 'eyes as large as saucers'. When walking, his feet make a loud splashing noise, like old shoes in a miry road, and hence the name 'Trash'.[239]

He also notes that the Gytrash in West Riding returns to water after being seen.

All over Europe, dogs of various kinds guard the entrance to the Underworld as in the Norse myths, where the dog, Garm, watches over.

In some Danish cases, the black dog is also connected to the wild hunt:

> In Kjøng south Funen, I often heard in the autumn of 1879 the hel hounds – that's what the old woman called them – it sounded up in the air like barking of dogs. At Køge they say that it is King Volmer who is out hunting with his dogs. In another part of Denmark, I don't remember which, I have heard it said, 'it is the heaven hounds who does the barking'.[240]

In the old Norse world, Hel is the realm of the dead and the Underworld, so the hellhound of folklore is undoubtedly connected back in time to the dogs of the Underworld.

References

1. Morris, Mark, *The Anglo-Saxons, A History of the Beginning of England*, 2021.
2. Varberg, Jeanette, *Viking, Ran, ild og Sværd* (Viking, Robbery, Fire and Swords), 2019.
3. *The Anglo-Saxon Chronicle*, Michael Swanton (ed. and trans.), 1996.
4. Lecouteux, Claude, *The Hidden History of Elves and Dwarfs: Avatars of Invisible Realms*, 2018.
5. Caesar, Julius, *Commentarii de Bello Gallico* (Conquest of Gaul), W. A. McDevitte and W. S. Bohn (trans.), 1st Edition. New York: Harper & Brothers, 1869.
6. Tacitus, *Germania.*
7. Strabo, *The Geography of Strabo.*
8. Lund, Allan A. *Tacitus Germania, forestillinger om Germania*, 2016.
9. Tacitus, *Germania.*
10. Unknown author, 'The Dätgen man and Iron Age sacrificial sights', November 26, 2023. https://bogbodyresource.com/2023/11/26/bog-bodies-at-schloss-gottorf-the-datgen-man-and-iron-age-sacrificial-sites/.
11. The Danish National Museum: https://nationalmuseet.dk/en.
12. Watson, 'Greig Digs suggest leafy village once saw Viking horrors', BBC, 2024.
13. Thietmar of Merseberg, *Ottonian Germany Thietmar's Chronicle*. Manchester University Press, 2001.
14. Bede, *Ecclesiastical History, Book 1 – A revised translation with introduction, life and notes by A. M. Sellar*. London: George Bell and Sons, 1907.
15. Hutton R., *The pagan religions of the ancient British Isles: their nature and legacy*. Blackwell, (1993.)
16. Sidonius Apollinaris, *Letters*, O. M. Dalton (trans.), Book VIII, Vol. 2, (1915), pp. 138–175.

17. Price, Neil, *The Viking Way: Religion and War in Late Iron Age Scandinavia*. Oxbow Books, 2002.
18. Tacitus, *Germania.*
19. Sturluson, Snorri, *Younger Edda: Gylfaginning*. Chicago: Scott, Foresman and Company, 1901.
20. Willibald, *The Life of St. Boniface*. Translation by George W. Robinson. Cambridge: Harvard University Press, 1906.
21. *Carolinian Chronicles: Royal Frankish Annals and Nithard's Histories*, Bernhard Walter Scholz (trans.). The University of Michigan Press, 1970.
22. Tid Museum Odense: https://tidmuseum.dk/.
23. Tacitus, *Germania.*
24. The Danish National Museum: https://nationalmuseet.dk/en.
25. Tacitus, *Germania.*
26. Sturluson, *Younger Edda: Gylfaginning.*
27. Tacitus, *Germania.*
28. Ibid.
29. Unknown Authors, *The Elder Edda of Saemund Sigfusson, Laxdæla Saga*. The Norroema Society, 1906.
30. Roskilde ship Museum: https://www.vikingeskibsmuseet.dk/en/.
31. Unknown Authors, *The Elder Edda.*
32. Price, *The Viking Way*, p. 64.
33. Ulriksen, Jens, *Vikingetidens gravskik*, (The burial costumes of the Viking Age) Kuml, 2011.
34. Saxo Grammaticus, *Gesta Danorum: History of the Danes*. Project Gutenberg English translation: https://www.gutenberg.org/files/1150/1150-h/1150-h.htm.
35. Ibid.
36. Sturluson, Snorri, *Egil's Skalagrim Saga.*
37. Unknown author, *Hervarar saga ok Heiðreks* (Hervor's Saga).
38. Grammaticus, *Gesta Danorum.*
39. Kamp, Jens, *Danske Folkeminder* (Danish Folk Memories), 1877.
40. *Danmarks Nationallexicon Nordisk mytologi*. (Danish National Encyclopedia of Nordic Mythology.)
41. Kristensen, Evald Tang, *Danske Sagn Som De Har Lydt I Folkemunde* (Danish Legends As They Have Been Told), 1892–1901,
42. Grammaticus, *Gesta Danorum: Bjarkemál.*
43. Sturluson, *Egil's Skalagrim's Saga.*
44. Bede, *Ecclesiastical History.*
45. Sturluson, *Younger Edda: Skáldskaparmál.*

46. van Dijk, Evelin, Ingar, Gundersen, Mørkestøl, de Bode, Anna, Høeg Helge, Loftsgarden, Ketil, Iversen, Frode Timmerech, Claudia, Jungclaus, Johann, Krüger, Kirsten, *Climatic and social impact in Scandinavia following the 536 and 540 CE Volcanic double event.*
47. Sturluson, *Younger Edda.*
48. Medieval fact sheet, Kirkby Stephen Church: https://aw-history.co.uk/information.
49. Sturluson, *Younger Edda: Skáldskaparmál.*
50. Ibid.
51. Sturluson, *Younger Edda: Gylfaginning.*
52. Unknown author, *Elder Edda: Völuspa,*
53. Ibid.
54. Sturluson, *Younger Edda: Gylfaginning.*
55. Unknown author Darraðarljóð (English translation – Old Norse and Viking Chants). https://lyricstranslate.com/en/darradarljod-dorruds-song.html.
56. Purser, Philip A., *Her Syndan Wælcyrian: Illuminating the Form and Function of the Valkyrie-Figure in the Literature, Mythology, and Social Consciousness of Anglo-Saxon England.* Georgia State University, (2013)
57. Sturluson, *Younger Edda: Skáldskaparmál.*
58. Ibid
59. Ibid
60. Ibid
61. Unknown author, *Elder Edda: Hávámál.*
62. Ibid.
63. Grammaticus, *Gesta Danorum.*
64. Glover, Andrew R., *The Music and 'Scopic' (Bardic/Skaldic) Elements of our Anglo-Saxon Ancestors.* Medievalist.Net, 2013.
65. Caesar, *Commentarii de Bello Gallico.*
66. Ibrahim ibn Ahmed at-Tartuschi (he visited Haithabu, a Danish trading town).
67. Sturluson, Snorri, *Heimskringla* (Haakon the Good's Saga).
68. Unknown author, *Hervarar saga ok Heiðreks* (Hervor's Saga).
69. Þórðarson, Sigvatr, *Austrfararvísur.*
70. Sturluson, *Younger Edda: Gylfaginning.*
71. Sturluson, *Younger Edda: Skáldskaparmál.*
72. Sturluson, *Younger Edda: Gylfaginning.*
73. Ibid.

74. Grammaticus, *Gesta Danorum*.
75. Magnus, Olaus, *The History of the Nordic People*, 1555.
76. Kristensen, *Danske Sagn*.
77. Kamp, *Folketro*.
78. Ibid.
79. American Literature.com: 'The Lambton Worm'.
80. Leather, Ella Mary, *The Folklore of Herefordshire*. Logastone Press, 1973.
81. Sturluson, *Younger Edda: Gylfaginning*.
82. Ibid.
83. Ibid.
84. Unknown author, *Elder Edda: Grímnismál*.
85. Sturluson, *Younger Edda: Gylfaginning*.
86. Unknown author, *Egil's Saga*.
87. Unknown author, *Elder Edda: Helgakvida Hunningsbana I*.
88. Unknown author, *Elder Edda: Grímnismál*.
89. Unknown author, *Elder Edda Vafþrúðnismál*.
90. Unknown author, *Elder Edda: Völuspa*.
91. Sturluson, *Younger Edda: Gylfaginning*.
92. Ibid.
93. Ibid.
94. Sturluson, *Younger Edda: Skáldskaparmál*.
95. Ibid.
96. Sturluson, *Younger Edda: Gylfaginning*.
97. Grammaticus, *Gesta Danorum*.
98. Sturluson, *Younger Edda: Gylfaginning*.
99. Ibid.
100. Ibid.
101. Danish National Museum, Berserkers: https://en.natmus.dk/historical-knowledge/denmark/prehistoric-period-until-1050-ad/the-viking-age/weapons/berserkers/.
102. Flyvbjerg, Charlotte, Nielsen, Thomas Garm, 'En Odin-figur med ravne på hjelmen fundet på Fyn' (An Odin figure with raven on the helmet found on Funen), 2016. https://www.dr.dk/nyheder/regionale/fyn/en-odin-figur-med-ravne-paa-hjelmen-fundet-paa-fyn.
103. Hornklofi Þorbjǫrn Haraldskvæði a Skald quatrain (*c*.1035).
104. Possible author: Sturluson, Snorri, *Egill Skallagrímsson Saga*.
105. Sturluson, Snorri, *Heimskringla, Ynglinga Saga*.
106. Rose, Winnifred Hodge, An Anglo-Saxon Charm Against a Dwarf: Shapeshifting, Soul Theft, and Shamanic Healing, https://heathensoullore.

net/an-anglo-saxon-charm-against-a-dwarf-shapeshifting-soul-theft-and-shamanic-healing/.
107. Unknown author, *Elder Edda: Völuspa.*
108. Unknown author, *Elder Edda: Hávámál.*
109. Unknown author, *Elder Edda: Vafthrudnersmaal.*
110. Unknown author, *Elder Edda: Völuspa.*
111. Unknown author, *Elder Edda: Skírnismál.*
112. Unknown author, *Elder Edda: Hyndluljóð.*
113. Thietmar of Merseberg, *Thietmar of Merseberg's Chronicle.*
114. Adam of Bremen, *Gesta Hammaburgensis ecclesiae pontificum* (History of the Archbishops of Hamburg-Bremen). https://archive.org/stream/historyofarchbis00adam
115. 'The Stentoften Runestone, New Interpretation of the Inscription', The Skaldic Project: https://skaldic.org/.
116. Unknown author, *Elder Edda: Völuspa.*
117. Ibid.
118. Unknown author, *Elder Edda, Grímnísmál.*
119. A series of papers by W. Traill Dennison, published in the Scottish Antiquary. 'Orkney Folklore and Sea Myths'. (1893)
120. Kamp, Jens, *Folketro.*
121. Ibid.
122. Unknown author, *Elder Edda: Völuspa.*
123. Unknown author, *Elder Edda: Grímnismál.*
124. Unknown author, *Elder Edda: Hávámál.*
125. Unknown author, *Elder Edda: Skírnismál.*
126. Ibid.
127. Unknown author, *Elder Edda, Lokasenna.*
128. Þórðarson, Jon and Þórhallsson, Magnús, *The Saga of Olaf Geirstade Alf, Flateyjarbók.*
129. Dixon, J. H. *Chronicles and Stories of the Craven Dales*. Edmondson and Co., 1888.
130. Collins, William, *Ode on the Popular Superstitions of the Highlands of Scotland*, 1788.
131. Owen, Elias, *Welsh Folklore: A Collection of the Folktales and Legends of North Wales*. Woodhall, Minshull & Co. Oswestry & Wrexham, 1896.
132. Wright, Thomas, *Essays on Archaeological Subjects, and on Various Questions Connected With the History of Art, Science, and Literature in the Middle Ages*.

133. Kristensen, *Danske Sagn.*
134. Wright, *Essays on Archaeological Subjects.*
135. Atkinson, Rev. J. C., *Forty Years in a Moorland County, Reminiscence and Research in Danby in Cleveland*, 1891.
136. Gardela, Leszek, Bending, Sophia, Pentz, Peter (eds.), *The Norse Sorceress, Mind and Materiality in the Viking World.* Oxbow Books, 2023.
137. Thiele, Just Mathias, *Danmarks Folkesagn* (Denmark's Folklore). C. A. Reitzel, 1843.
138. Wright, *Essays on Archaeological Subjects.*
139. Kristensen, *Danske Sagn.*
140. Ibid.
141. Owen, *Welsh Folklore.*
142. *Brewer's Dictionary of Phrase and Fable*, 1898
143. Young, George, *History of Whitby.*
144. Atkinson, *Forty Years in a Moorland County.*
145. Ibid.
146. MacKenzie, *Scottish Folk-Lore.*
147. Briggs, M. K., *Origins of Fairies*, 1976.
148. Kristensen, *Danske Sagn.*
149. MacKenzie, *Scottish Folk-Lore.*
150. Keightley, Thomas, *The Fairy Mythology.*
151. Kristensen, *Danske Sagn.*
152. Owen, *Welsh Folklore.*
153. The Brothers Grimm, *German Mythology*, 1835.
154. Kristensen, *Danske Sagn.*
155. Campbell, *Popular Tales of the West Highlands.*
156. Kristensen, *Danske Sagn.*
157. Grimm, Jacob and Wilhelm, *Children's and Household Tales.*
158. Campbell, *Popular Tales of the West Highlands.*
159. Gardala, Leszek *et al.*, *The Norse Sorceress.*
160. Campbell, *Popular Tales of the West Highlands.*
161. Ælfric of Eynsham, *De falsis diis.*
162. Owen, *Welsh Folklore.*
163. Kristensen, *Danske Sagn.*
164. Urhskov, *Fynske Sagn.*
165. Owen, *Welsh Folklore.*
166. Worthington George Smith, *Man, the Primeval Savage.* University of Michigan, 1894.

167. Ulriksen, Jens, *From Kuml 2011— Vikingetidens gravskik i Danmark* (The burial costumes of the Viking age in Denmark).
168. Sikes, *British Goblins*.
169. Wright, *Rustic Speech and Folklore*.
170. Atkinson, *Forty Years in a Moorland County*.
171. Dennison, 'Orkney Folklore and Sea Myths'.
172. MacKenzie, *Wonder Tales from Scottish Myth and Legend*.
173. Moore, A. W., *The Folklore of the Isle of Man*, 1891.
174. MacKenzie, *Wonder Tales*.
175. Unknown author, *Egils Saga: Sonatorrek*.
176. Sturluson, Snorri, *Saga of St. Olaf* (Óláfs sögu ins Helga inni sérstöku).
177. *Ladnámabók: The Book of Settlements*. Hermann Pálsson and Paul Edwards (trans.), University of Manitoba, 1972.
178. Keightley, Thomas, *The Fairy Mythology*.
179. Dennison, 'Orkney Folklore and Sea Myths'.
180. MacKenzie, *Wonder Tales*.
181. Burne, Charlotte S., *What Folklore is, and How it is to be Collected*, 1896.
182. Collins, William, *Ode on the Popular Superstition of the Highlands of Scotland*.
183. Lauder, Thomas Dick, *Tales of the Highlands*.
184. Ibid.
185. Blantyre Simpson, Evelyn, *Folk-lore in Lowland Scotland*. London: J. M. Dent and company, 1908.
186. MacKenzie, *Scottish Folk-Lore*.
187. Kristensen, *Danske Sagn*.
188. Grimm, Jacob, *Deutche Mythologie*.
189. Kristensen, *Danske Sagn*.
190. Ibid.
191. Huldra Lore, https://art342s18. wordpress. com/wp-content/uploads/2018/05/huldra-content. pdf.
192. Ibid.
193. Hammershaimb, V. U., *Færøsk Anthologi*. København, 1891. *Heimskringla*.
194. Unknown author, *Elder Edda: Grímnismál*.
195. Sturluson, *Younger Edda: Gylfaginning*.
196. Ibid.
197. Unknown author, *Elder Edda: Grímnismál*.
198. *Annals of St. Neots*.

199. *Encomium Emmae Reginae*. Alistair Campbell (ed.), London: Royal Historical Society. (1949). https://archive.org/stream/in.ernet.dli.2015.185337/2015.185337.Encomium-Emmae-Reginae_djvu.txt.
200. Unknown author, *Orkney Saga*.
201. Sax, Boria, 'Medievalism, Paganism, and the Tower Ravens', *Pomegranate: The International Journey of Pagan Studies*, 2007.
202. Mackindlay, James M., *Folklore of Scottish Lochs and Springs*. Glasgow: William Hodge and Co., 1893.
203. Leather, Ella Mary, *The Folk-lore of Herefordshire*. Logaston Press, 2022.
204. Kristensen, *Danske Sagn*.
205. Ibid.
206. Spenberg, Thomas, *The Dialect and Folklore of Northamptonshire*. John Russell Smith, London, 1851.
207. Leather, *The folk-lore of Herefordshire*.
208. Trolle, Johannes, *Flora og folketro, især i Holbæk amt, historiske aarbøger* (Plants and Folklore Especially in Holbæk District), 1953.
209. Kamp, *Folketro*.
210. Vickery, *Oxford Dictionary of Plant-lore*.
211. Leather, *The folk-lore of Herefordshire*.
212. Lidegaard, Mads, *Danske træer i sagn og overtro* (Danish Trees in Legends and Beliefs). Arnold Busch, 1996.
213. Ibid.
214. Atkinson, *Forty Years in a Moorland County*.
215. Kristensen, *Danske Sagn*.
216. Hartland, Sidney. *English Fairies and Other Folktales*, 1906.
217. Mason, Marilyn, *Magic in the Park*. Friends of Richmond Park, 2010.
218. Kristensen, *Danske Sagn*.
219. Campbell, John Gregorsen, *Superstition of the Highlands and Islands of Scotland. Glasgow*, James MacLehose and Sons, 1900.
220. Vickery, *Oxford Dictionary of Plant-lore*.
221. Duncan, Leland L., *Folk-Lore Gleanings from County Leitrim*. Blatter Press, 2012.
222. Atkinson, *Forty Years in a Moorland County*.
223. Rasmussen, Jens, *Smaatræk fra Vestfyn* (Small stories from West Funen).
224. Bircherod, Jacob, *Folketro og festskik, særligt fra Fyn* (Folk beliefs and Party Costumes, especially from Funen), 1734.
225. Vickery, *Oxford Dictionary of Plant-lore*.
226. Hutchinson, William, *A view of Northumberland with an excursion to the abbey of Mailross in Scotland*. Northumberland Archives, (1778).

227. Burne, Charlotte S., *What Folklore is, and How it is to be Collected*, 1896.
228. Larringson, Carolyne, *The Land of the Green Man*. Bloomsbury Publishing, 2015.
229. Vickery, *Oxford Dictionary of Plant-lore*.
230. Ibid
231. Kamp, *Folketro*.
232. Vickery, *Oxford Dictionary of Plant-lore*.
233. Fynhistorie.dk. https://www.fynhistorie.dk/node/6197.
234. Vickery, *Oxford Dictionary of Plant-lore*.
235. Kamp, *Folketro*.
236. William A. Dutt, *Highways and Byways in East Anglia*. London, New York, MacMillian and Co., Limited, 1901.
237. Leather, *The folk-lore of Herefordshire*.
238. Brontë, Charlotte, *Jane Eyre*.
239. Horsfall, Turner, *Yorkshire Folklore Journal*, 1888.
240. Kamp, *Folketro*.

Bibliography

Adam of Bremen, *Gesta Hammaburgensis Ecclesiae Pontificum* (The deeds of the bishops of Hamburg). https://archive.org/details/gestahammaburgen00adamuoft/page/n5/mode/2up.

Anonymous Author, *The Life of Saint Columba, Abbot, and Apostle of the Northern Picts*. John Murphy (trans.), Project Gutenberg eBook. (2012)

Atkinson, Rev. J. C., *Forty Years in a Moorland County, Reminiscence and Research in Danby in Cleveland.* (1891)

Bede, *Ecclesiastical History, Book 1.*A revised translation with introduction, life and notes by A. M. Sellar. London, George Bell and Sons. (1907)

Blantyre Simpson, Evelyn, *Folk-lore in Lowland Scotland.* London: J.M. Dent and Company. (1908)

Brewer's Dictionary of Phrase and Fable. (1898)

Caesar, Julius, *Commentarii de Bello Gallico* (Conquest of Gaul). W. A. McDevitte and W. S. Bohn (trans.), 1st Edition, New York: Harper & Brothers. (1869)

Campbell, John Gregorsen, *Superstition of the Highlands and Islands of Scotland.* Glasgow: James MacLehose and Sons. (1900)

Carolinian Chronicles: Royal Frankish Annals and Nithard's Histories. Bernhard Walter Scholz (trans.), The University of Michigan Press. (1970)

Collins, William, *Ode on the Popular Superstitions of the Highlands of Scotland.* (1788)

Dennison, W. Traill. 'Orkney Folklore and Sea Myths', *The Scottish Antiquary, or, Northern Notes and Queries 7.* (1893)

Diodorus Siculus, *Library of History.* Vol. VII., Loeb Classical Library. (1952)

Dixon, J. H., *Chronicles and Stories of the Craven Dales.* Edmondson and Co. (1888)

Duncan, Leland L., *Folk-Lore Gleanings from County Leitrim.* Blatter Press. (2012)

Encomium Emmae Reginae. Alistair Campbell (ed.), London: Royal Historical Society. (1949) *https://archive.org/stream/in.ernet.dli.2015.185337/2015.185337.Encomium-Emmae-Reginae_djvu.txt.*

Gardela, Leszek, Bending, Sophia, Pentz, Peter (eds.), *The Norse Sorceress, Mind and Materiality in the Viking World.* Oxbow books. (2023)

Horsfall, Turner, *Yorkshire Folklore Journal.* (1888)

Huldra Lore, https://art342s18.wordpress.com/wp-content/uploads/2018/05/huldra-content.pdf.

Hunt, Robert (ed.), *King Arthur in the Form of a Chough.* London: John Camden Hotten. (1965)

Hutchinson, William. *A view of Northumberland with an excursion to the abbey of Mailross in Scotland.* Northumberland Archives. (1778)

Hutton R., *The Pagan Religions of the Ancient British Isles: Their Nature and Legacy.* Blackwell. (1993)

Ladnámabók: The Book of Settlements. Hermann Pálsson and Paul Edwards (trans.), University of Manitoba. (1972)

Larrington, Carolyne, *The Land of the Green Man.* Bloomsbury Publishing. (2015)

Leather, Ella Mary, *The Folk-lore of Herefordshire.* Logaston Press. (2022)

Lecouteux, Claude, *The Hidden History of Elves and Dwarfs: Avatars of Invisible Realms.* Inner Traditions. (2018)

Livius (Livy), Titus, *The History of Rome, Book 23.* Rev. Canon Roberts (ed.) J. M. Dent & Sons, Ltd., London. (1905)

MacKenzie, Donald Alexander, *Scottish Folk-Lore and Folk Life: Studies in Race, Culture and Tradition.* Blackie. (1935)

Mackindlay, James M., *Folklore of Scottish Lochs and Springs.* Glasgow: William Hodge and Co. (1893)

Mason, Marilyn, *Magic in the Park.* Friends of Richmond Park. (2010)

Moore, A.W., *The Folklore of the Isle of Man.* (1891)

Morris, Mark, *The Anglo-Saxons: A History of the Beginning of England.* Hutchinson/Windmill Books Ltd. (2021)

Owen, Elias, *Welsh Folklore: A Collection of the Folktales and Legends of North Wales.* Woodhall, Minshull & Co. Oswestry & Wrexham. (1896)

Pliny the Elder, *Natural History.* Translator John Bostock. (2018)

Price, Neil, *The Viking Way: Religion and War in Late Iron Age Scandinavia.* Oxbow Books. (2002)

Sax, Boria, 'Medievalism, Paganism, and the Tower Ravens', *Pomegranate: The International Journey of Pagan Studies.* (2007) https://www.researchgate.net/publication/240764250_Medievalism_Paganism_and_the_Tower_Ravens.

Schneidau, Lisa, *River Folk Tales of Britain and Ireland.* History Press Ltd. (2022)

Sidonius Apollinaris, *Letters.* O. M. Dalton (trans.). Book VIII, Vol. 2. (1915)

Speidel, Leo, Silva, Marina, Booth, Thomas, Raffield, Ben, Anastasiadou, Kyriaki, Barrington, Christopher, Götherström, Anders, Heather, Peter, Skoglund, Pontus, 'High-Resolution Genomic History of Early Medieval Europe', *Nature.* (2025)

Strabo, *The Geography of Strabo.* Literally Translated, With Notes. The First Six Books By H. C. Hamilton, Esq. The Remainder By W. Falconer, M.A. London: Henry G. Bohn. (1857)

Sturluson, Snorri, *Younger Edda.* Chicago: Scott, Foresman and Company (1901).

Tacitus, *Germania.* The Oxford translations with notes from Edward Brooks Jr. (2013)

The Brothers Grimm, *German Mythology.* (1835)

Thietmar of Merseberg, *Ottonian Germany Thietmar's Chronicle.* Manchester University Press. (2001)

Þórðarson, Jon and Þórhallsson, Magnús, *The Saga of Olaf Geirstade Alf, Flateyjarbók.*

Unknown Authors, *The Elder Edda of Saemund Sigfusson.* The Norroema Society. (1906)

Various, *The Anglo-Saxon Chronicle.* Translated and edited by Michael Swanton. (1996)

William A. Dutt, *Highways and Byways in East Anglia.* London: New York, Macmillan and Co., Ltd. (1901)

Willibald, *The Life of St. Boniface.* Translation by George W. Robinson. Cambridge: Harvard University Press. (1906)

Worthington George Smith, *Man, the Primeval Savage.* University of Michigan. (1894)

Wright, Thomas, *Essays on Archaeological Subjects, and on Various Questions Connected With the History of Art, Science, and Literature in the Middle Ages.*

Danish Sources

Bircherod, Jacob, *Folketro og festskik, særligt fra Fyn* (Folk beliefs and Party Costumes, Especially from Funen). (1734)

Danmarks Nationallexicon Nordisk mytologi. Danish National Encyclopedia of Nordic Mythology.

Fynhistorie.dk. https://www.fynhistorie.dk/node/6197.

Hammershaimb, V. U., *Færøsk Anthologi,* København. (1891)

Ibrahim ibn Ahmed at-Tartuschi (Tenth-century merchant and traveller who visited Haithabu, a Danish trading town, and wrote an account in Arabic of his travels).

Kamp, Jens, *Danske Folkeminder* (Danish Folk Memories). (1877)

Kristensen, Evald Tang, *Danske Sagn Som De Har Lydt I Folkemunde* (Danish Legends As They Have Been Told). (1892–1901)

Lidegaard, Mads, *Danske træer i sagn og overtro* (Danish Trees in Legends and Beliefs). Arnold Busch. (1996)

Lund, Allan A. *Tacitus Germania, forestillinger om Germani.* (2016)

Rasmussen, Jens, *Smaatræk fra Vestfyn* (Small stories from West Funen).

Roskilde Ship Museum: https://www.vikingeskibsmuseet.dk/en/.

Sturluson, Snorri, *Heimskringla: History of the Kings of Norway.*

Thiele, Just Mathias, *Danmarks Folkesagn* (Denmark's folklore). C.A. Reitzel. (1843)

Tid Museum Odense: https://tidmuseum.dk/.

Trolle, Johannes, *Flora og folketro, især i Holbæk amt, historiske aarbøger* (Plants and Folklore Especially in Holbæk District). (1953)

Ulriksen, Jens, *From Kuml 2011- Vikingetidens gravskik i Danmark* (The Burial Costumes of the Viking age in Denmark).

Urhskov, Anders, *Fynske Sagn* (Folktales from Funen). P. Haase og søns forlag. (1929).

Varberg, Jeanette, *Viking, Ran, ild og Sværd* (Viking, Robbery, Fire and Swords). (2019)

Unknown author *The Dätgen man and Iron Age sacrificial sights*, November 26, 2023. https://bogbodyresource.com/2023/11/26/bog-bodies-at-schloss-gottorf-the-datgen-man-and-iron-age-sacrificial-sites/